EYEWITNESS *TRAVEL* GUIDES

HEBREW
PHRASE BOOK

A DK Publishing Book
www.dk.com

A DK PUBLISHING BOOK

www.dk.com

Compiled by Lexus Ltd with Fania Oz-Salzberger and Roberta Rosen-Kerler

First American Edition, 1999

2 4 6 8 10 9 7 5 3

Published in the United States by DK Publishing, Inc.
95 Madison Avenue, New York, New York 10016

DK Publishing books are available at special discounts for bulk purchases
for sales promotions or premiums. Special editions, including personalized
covers, excerpts of existing guides, and corporate imprints can be created in
large quantities for specific needs. For more information, contact Special
Markets Dept./DK Publishing, Inc./95 Madison Ave./New York,
NY 10016/Fax: 800-600-9098.

Library of Congress Cataloging-in-Publication Data
Hebrew phrase book/ [compiled] by Lexus Ltd. with Fania Oz-
Salzberger and Roberta Rosen-Kerler.
    p.   cm. -- (Eyewitness travel guides)
    ISBN 0–7894–4186–1 (alk. paper)
    1. Hebrew language--Conversation and phrase books--English.
I. Oz-Salzberger, Fania.   II. Rosen-Kerler, Roberta.   III. Lexus
(Firm)   IV. Series.
PJ4573.H44 1999
492.4'83421--dc21   98–53865
                                 CIP

Picture Credits

Jacket: CORBIS IMAGES: Michael Nicholson spine; Richard T Nowitz top left;
DK: Clive Streeter top right; EDDIE GERALD: center above, center below,
center left, center right, bottom left, bottom right, bottom center, back cover
left; ROBERT HARDING PICTURE LIBRARY: E Simanor back cover right.

Printed and bound in Italy by Printer Trento Srl.

CONTENTS

PREFACE

This *Eyewitness Travel Guide Phrase Book* has been compiled
by experts to meet the general needs of tourists and business
travelers. Arranged under headings such as Hotels, Driving,
and so forth, the Hebrew words and phrases you may need are
also printed in familiar roman letters, following an easy-to-use
pronunciation system that is fully explained in the Introduction
on pages 5–7.

Most sections of this book include boxes headed *Things You'll
See*, which list the common words, signs, notices, etc., that you
may see in Hebrew script, while the boxes headed *Things You'll
Hear* contain typical replies to questions you may ask during
your trip.

A 1,900-line mini-dictionary will help you form additional
phrases, and the extensive menu guide lists approximately 250
dishes or methods of cooking and presentation. Guidance on
aspects of the Israeli way of life, customs, and holidays will be
found under the heading Cross-Cultural Notes.

Eyewitness Travel Guides are recognized as the world's best
travel guides. Each title features specially commissioned color
photographs, cutaways of major buildings, 3-D aerial views,
and detailed maps, plus information on sights, events, hotels,
restaurants, shopping, and entertainment.

Eyewitness Travel Guides titles include:

Amsterdam · Australia · Sydney · Budapest · California · Florida
Hawaii · New York · San Francisco & Northern California
France · Loire Valley · Paris · Provence · Great Britain
London · Ireland · Dublin · Greece: Athens & the Mainland
The Greek Islands · Istanbul · Italy · Florence & Tuscany
Naples · Rome · Sardinia · Venice & the Veneto · Moscow
St. Petersburg · Portugal · Lisbon · Prague · Spain · Madrid
Seville & Andalusia · Thailand · Vienna · Warsaw

INTRODUCTION

PRONUNCIATION

When reading the imitated pronunciation, stress the part that is underlined. Pronounce each syllable as if it formed part of an English word, and you will be understood. Remember the points below, and your pronunciation will be even closer to the correct Hebrew:

ai	as in "Thai"
ay	as in "pay"
e	as in "bed"
er	as in "where"
g	as in "good"
KH	a gutteral "ch" as in the Scottish word "loch"
o	as in "hot" (remember that words such as **lo** are not pronounced "low")
u	as in "pull"
ZH	"s" as in "leisure"
'	signifies a guttural, "throaty" sound at the start of the next syllable

The mini-dictionary provides the Hebrew translations using the imitated pronunciation so that you can read the words without reference to the Hebrew alphabet. The abbreviations (m) and (f) used in this book indicate the forms to be used by a male or female speaker or, in the case of an adjective, the forms to be used when referring to a male or female. The forms to be used when speaking to a man or a woman are indicated by (to a man) and (to a woman) following the words applying to each.

Hebrew has no vowels and only an experienced reader can know whether the written character is pronounced like a, e, i, o, or u. You may sometimes come across texts—the Hebrew Bible, for example, as well as children's books—that have a vowel system consisting of dots and lines, called **nikud** (vocalization or vowel marks). However, most of the everyday written Hebrew that you will encounter will not have vowel sounds shown.

"The" in Hebrew is **ha-** added to the beginning of the noun and also to the beginning of both the adjective and the noun when both are used. There is no indefinite article (a, an) in Hebrew.

THE HEBREW ALPHABET

The first letter of the alphabet, א, is the equivalent of the English letter "a," but it can be pronounced in any of the following ways:

a	as in "arm"
e	as in "elf"
i	as in "inn"
o	as in "order"
oo	as in "ooze"

Most other letters used in this book have direct equivalents in the English alphabet:

א	a (also e, i, etc., see above)
ב	b or v
ג	g as in "good"
ד	d
ה	h
ו	v or o as in "hot" or u as in "pull"
ז	z
ח	KH like "ch" in "loch"
ט	t
י	y or i
כ	KH like "ch" in "loch" or k
ל	l

מ   m

נ   n

ס   s

ע   pronounced like א but from the back of the throat

פ   p or f

צ   tz as in "Ritz"

ק   k

ר   r

ש   sh as in "shop," but sometimes pronounced s

ת   t

The following letters have a different form (but the same sound) when appearing at the end of a word:

letter	end of word form	
כ	ך	KH
מ	ם	m
נ	ן	n
פ	ף	f
צ	ץ	tz

Although the following do not appear in this book, you might see them occasionally:

וּ   u as in "pull"

וֹ   o as in "hot"

כ   k

ב   b

פ   p

CROSS-CULTURAL NOTES

Many aspects of Israeli society can appear, to a first-time visitor, surprisingly Western. In terms of technology, communications, and everyday facilities, Israel resembles European countries. Tel Aviv is a modern, bustling metropolis, where art, theater, and movies thrive. Jerusalem displays a far more complex picture: it is a fascinating mixture of old and new, with traditional Arab and orthodox Jewish neighborhoods maintaining a tense coexistence alongside the secular, modern parts of the city. The **kibbutzim** (plural of **kibbutz**, a communal settlement) and the **moshavim** (cooperative settlements) are interesting social experiments, combining socialist and liberal values, and based upon modern farming and industry.

Most Israelis, regardless of their ethnic or political affiliations, are friendly, informal, and talkative. Many speak some English, but would be delighted to hear your Hebrew. You'll find that, even with strangers, on public transportation and in stores, for example, Israelis do not stand on ceremony. Physical gestures are more common than in northern Europe. First names are universally used, except in extremely formal situations. A great deal can be done without a jacket or a tie, and dress is usually casual and well-adapted to the climate. There are few inhibitions in conversation: even total strangers would not hesitate to embark on a political discussion. Your views may be vehemently contested, but you are welcome to put them forward. Personal matters are discussed less freely than in the US but more than in England.

Despite this openness, tact and common sense are recommended when encountering the sensitive areas of Israeli society: the Jewish majority originates from over one hundred countries, from Poland to Ethiopia. It is extremely varied in its lifestyle, attitude toward religion, and political outlook. Israel's Muslim and Christian Arabs (about 18% of the population), and the Palestinians living in the occupied West Bank and

Gaza Strip, also display a variety of customs and opinions. It would be useful to acquaint yourself with the current state of debate on the Israeli-Arab conflict. Generally speaking, the Israeli Left has traditionally supported a territorial compromise and more attention to civil rights, while the Right is more concerned with the value of the occupied territories for Israel's security and its Jewish cultural-religious identity.

Israel itself is, on the whole, safe for travelers and tourists, but not all parts of Jerusalem or Israel's occupied territories are equally safe. For women, modest dress is advisable in the Arab areas and in the orthodox Jewish neighborhoods.

Israel's religious establishment is politically more powerful than most of its Western counterparts, even though most Israelis are avowedly secular. The religion's mark on everyday life is most noticeable with regard to the Sabbath and Jewish dietary rules. The Jewish Sabbath lasts from Friday afternoon to early Saturday evening. Public transportation is very limited at this time: banks, stores, and some restaurants are closed. It's advisable to seek advice locally and plan accordingly. However, in most areas, theaters, movie theaters, restaurants, and cafés remain open.

Kosher dietary rules apply in many restaurants and most hotels. Basically, this means that meat and milk products cannot be eaten together, that pork and shellfish are not served, and that your hotel will serve a cold buffet on Saturday. Alcoholic drinks are available—Israel produces its own wine and beers, but their consumption is far less central to social life than in the US. To Israelis, a "drink" is most likely to mean a soft drink, unless "alcoholic" is explicitly stated.

THE JEWISH CALENDAR

Although the Jewish calendar varies by a few days each year, the broad pattern is the same: **Av** is July/August, **Elul** is August/September, etc.

Jewish Months

Tishrei	תשרי	_tishray_
Heshvan	חשון	_KHeshvan_
Kislev	כסלו	_kislev_
Teveth	טבת	_tevet_
Shevat	שבט	_shvat_
Adar*	אדר	_adar_
Nisan	ניסן	_nisan_
Iyar	אייר	_iyar_
Sivan	סיון	_sivan_
Tammuz	תמוז	_tamuz_
Av	אב	_av_
Elul	אלול	_elul_

* Every four years, a thirteenth month, **Adar Bet** is added between **Adar** and **Nisan** to adjust the Jewish year to the general calendar.

Jewish Festivals

Jewish New Year ראש השנה _rosh ha-shana_
– literally, "head of the year," 1 and 2 Tishrei (in September or October)

Yom Kippur יום כפור _yom kipur_
– means "the Day of Atonement" on 10 Tishrei (usually in October)

Feast of Tabernacles סוכות _sukot_
– 15–21 Tishrei (usually in October)

Hanukah חנוכה *KHanuka*
– commemorates the victory of the Maccabees and falls around Christmas time

Tu B'Shevat טו בשבט *tu b'shvat*
– called "the New Year of Trees," celebrating the first signs of spring

Purim פורים *purim*
– festival of rejoicing, usually in March, associated with the book of Esther and relating to the Jewish exile in Persia

Passover פסח *pesaKH*
– 15–21 Nisan, around Easter time

Memorial Day יום הזכרון *yom ha-zikaron*
– Day of Remembrance, preceding Independence Day

Independence Day יום העצמאות *yom ha-'atzma'ut*
– usually in April or May

Feast of Weeks שבועות *shavu'ot*
– harvest festival, usually in May or June

Fast of Av תשעה באב *tish'a be-'av*
– commemorates the Destruction of the Jewish Temple, usually in August

USEFUL EVERYDAY PHRASES

Yes/no
כן / לא
ken/lo

Thank you
תודה
toda

No thank you
לא תודה
lo toda

Please
בבקשה
bevakasha

I don't understand
אני לא מבין / מבינה
ani lo mevin (m)/*mevina* (f)

Do you speak English/French/German?
אתה מדבר אנגלית / צרפתית / גרמנית?
ata medaber anglit/tzorfatit/germanit? (to a man)

את מדברת אנגלית / צרפתית / גרמנית?
at medaberet anglit/tzorfatit/germanit? (to a woman)

I can't speak Hebrew
אני לא מדבר / מדברת עברית
ani lo medaber (m)/*medaberet* (f) *ivrit*

I don't know
אני לא יודע/יודעת
ani lo yo*de*'a (m)/yo*da*'at (f)

Please speak more slowly
בבקשה לדבר יותר לאט
bevakasha leda*ber* yoter le*'at*

Please write it down for me
בבקשה לכתוב את זה בשבילי
bevakasha liKHtov et zeh bishvi*li*

My name is . . .
שמי ...
shmi . . .

Pleased to meet you
נעים מאד
na*'im* me*od*

Good morning
בקר טוב
boker tov

Good evening
ערב טוב
erev tov

Good night
לילה טוב
*lai*la tov

Good-bye

שלום

shalom

See you later

להתראות

lehitra'ot

How are you?

מה שלומך?

ma shlomkHA? (to a man)

מה שלומך?

ma shlomekH? (to a woman)

Excuse me, please

סליחה בבקשה

slikHa bevakasha

Sorry!

סליחה!

slikHa!

I'm very sorry

אני מאד מצטער/מצטערת

ani meod mitzta'er (m)/*mitzta'eret* (f)

Can you help me?

אפשר לעזור לי?

efshar la'azor li?

Can you tell me . . .?
אפשר להגיד לי ...?
efshar lehagid li . . .?

May I have . . .?
אפשר לקבל ...?
efshar lekabel . . .?

Is there . . . here?
האם יש ... כאן?
ha'im yesh kan . . .?

Where can I get . . .?
איפה אפשר להשיג ...?
ayfo efshar lehasig . . .?

How much is it?
כמה זה עולה?
kama zeh oleh?

What time is it?
מה השעה?
ma ha-sha'a?

I must go now
אני צריך/צריכה ללכת עכשיו
ani tzariкн (m)/tzriкна (f) laleкнet aкнshav

I'm lost
הלכתי לאיבוד
halaкнti le'ibud

Cheers! (*toast*)

לחיים!

le-<u>KH</u>ayim!

Do you take credit cards?

אתם מקבלים כרטיסי אשראי?

a<u>tem</u> meka<u>blim</u> karti<u>say</u> ash<u>rai</u>?

Where is the restroom?

איפה השירותים?

<u>ay</u>fo ha-sheru<u>tim</u>?

Go away!

לך מפה!

le<u>KH</u> mi-<u>po</u>!

Excellent!

מצוין!

metzu<u>yan</u>!

THINGS YOU'LL HEAR

<u>ani</u> lo me<u>vin</u> (*m*)/me<u>vina</u> (*f*)	I don't understand
<u>ani</u> lo yo<u>de</u>'a (*m*)/yo<u>da</u>'at (*f*)	I don't know
be-'e<u>met</u>?	Really? Is that so?
bevaka<u>sha</u>	You're welcome; please
im yir<u>tzeh</u> ha-<u>shem</u>	God willing
lehitra'<u>ot</u>	See you later
ma nish<u>ma</u>?	How's it going?
ma shlom<u>KHa</u>? (*to a man*)	How are you?
ma shlom<u>eKH</u>? (*to a woman*)	How are you?

→

16

naKHon	That's right
<u>rega</u> e<u>KHad</u>!	Just a minute!
sha<u>bat</u> sha<u>lom</u>	Good Sabbath (said on Friday evening and Saturday)
sha<u>lom</u>	Good-bye
sha<u>lom</u>, na<u>'im</u> me<u>od</u>	Hello, pleased to meet you
sha<u>vu</u>'a tov	Have a good week (said on Saturday night)
sli<u>KHa</u>?	Excuse me?
to<u>da</u>	Thanks
tov to<u>da</u> ve-a<u>ta</u>? *(to a man)*	Very well, thank you—and you?
tov to<u>da</u> ve-<u>at</u>? *(to a woman)*	Very well, thank you—and you?
zeh lo mesha<u>ne</u>	It doesn't matter
zehi<u>rut</u>!	Be careful!

THINGS YOU'LL SEE

הכניסה חינם	ha-kni<u>sa</u> KHinam	admission free
דירה להשכרה	di<u>ra</u> le-haskara	apartment for rent
חוף הים	KHof ha-<u>yam</u>	beach
באר שבע	be'<u>er</u> <u>she</u>va	Beer Sheva
קופה	ku<u>pa</u>	cash desk
כנסיה	knesi<u>ya</u>	church
מרכז העיר	mer<u>kaz</u> ha'<u>ir</u>	city center
סגור	sa<u>gur</u>	closed
סגור לתקופת החגים	sa<u>gur</u> le-teku<u>fat</u> ha-KHagi<u>m</u>	closed for the holiday period
הנחה	hanaKHa	discount
מי שתיה	may shti<u>ya</u>	drinking water →

17

אילת	ay<u>lat</u>	Eilat
מעלית	ma'a<u>lit</u>	elevator
יציאת חרום	yetzi'<u>at</u> кнe<u>rum</u>	emergency exit
תפוס	ta<u>fus</u>	engaged, reserved
כניסה	k<u>nisa</u>	entrance
יציאה	yetzi'<u>a</u>	exit
אסור	a<u>sur</u>	forbidden
למכירה	le-me<u>кнira</u>	for sale
חיפה	<u>кнaifa</u>	Haifa
צ.ה.ל.	<u>tzahal</u>	Israeli Defense Forces
ירושלים	yerusha<u>lay</u>im	Jerusalem
כשר	ka<u>sher</u>	kosher
גברים	gva<u>rim</u>	men's restroom
שטח צבאי	<u>she</u>taкн tzva'<u>i</u>	military zone
מסגד	mis<u>gad</u>	mosque
הכניסה אסורה	ha-k<u>nisa</u> a<u>surah</u>	no admission
אין כניסה	ayn k<u>nisa</u>	no entry
העיר העתיקה	ha-'<u>ir</u> ha-a<u>tika</u>	old city
פתוח	pa<u>tu</u>aкн	open
פרטי	pra<u>ti</u>	private
משוך	me<u>shoкн</u>	pull
דחוף	de<u>кнof</u>	push
שירותים	she<u>rutim</u>	restrooms
עתיקות	ati<u>kot</u>	ruins, antiques
מבצע, מכירה	miv<u>tza</u>, me<u>кнira</u>	sale
שקט	<u>she</u>ket	silence, quiet

→

חפץ חשוד	KHefetz KHashud	suspicious object
בית כנסת	bayt kneset	synagogue
תל אביב	tel aviv	Tel Aviv
פנוי	panui	vacant
שעות ביקור	she'ot bikur	visiting hours
צבע טר	tzeva tari	wet paint
ינשים	nashim	women's restroom

DAYS, MONTHS, SEASONS

Sunday	יום ראשון	yom ri<u>sh</u>on
Monday	יום שני	yom she<u>ni</u>
Tuesday	יום שלישי	yom shli<u>shi</u>
Wednesday	יום רביעי	yom revi'i
Thursday	יום חמישי	yom кHami<u>shi</u>
Friday	יום שישי	yom shi<u>shi</u>
Saturday	שבת	sha<u>bat</u>
January	ינואר	<u>yanuar</u>
February	פברואר	<u>feb</u>ruar
March	מרס, מרץ	mars, mertz
April	אפריל	<u>april</u>
May	מאי	mai
June	יוני	<u>yu</u>ni
July	יולי	<u>yu</u>li
August	אוגוסט	<u>o</u>gust
September	ספטמבר	sep<u>tem</u>ber
October	אוקטובר	ok<u>to</u>ber
November	נובמבר	no<u>vem</u>ber
December	דצמבר	det<u>zem</u>ber
Spring	אביב	a<u>viv</u>
Summer	קיץ	<u>ka</u>yitz
Fall	סתו	stav
Winter	חורף	KHo<u>ref</u>

Christmas Eve	ערב חג המולד	_erev KHag ha-mo<u>lad</u>
Christmas	חג המולד	KHag ha-mo<u>lad</u>
New Year's Eve	ערב ראש השנה האזרחית	_erev rosh ha-sha<u>na</u> ha-ezraKHit
New Year's Day	ראש השנה האזרחית	rosh ha-sha<u>na</u> ha-ezraKHit
Easter	חג הפסחא	KHag ha-<u>pas</u>KHa
Ramadan (_Muslim month of fasting_)	רמדן	rama<u>dan</u>

NUMBERS, TIME

The numbers below are given in the feminine form. This is the form you are most likely to need since it is used for counting and telling time.

0	אפס	_efes_
1	אחת	_aKHat_
2	שתיים	_shtayim_
3	שלוש	_shalosh_
4	ארבע	_arba_
5	חמש	_KHamesh_
6	שש	_shesh_
7	שבע	_sheva_
8	שמונה	_shmoneh_
9	תשע	_tesha_
10	עשר	_eser_
11	אחת עשרה	_aKHat esreh_
12	שתים עשרה	_shtaym esreh_
13	שלוש עשרה	_shlosh esreh_
14	ארבע עשרה	_arba esreh_
15	חמש עשרה	_KHamesh esreh_
16	שש עשרה	_shesh esreh_
17	שבע עשרה	_shva esreh_
18	שמונה עשרה	_shmoneh esreh_
19	תשע עשרה	_tesha esreh_
20	עשרים	_esrim_
21	עשרים ואחת	_esrim ve-aKHat_
22	עשרים ושתיים	_esrim ve-shtayim_

30	שלושים	shlo_shim_
31	שלושים ואחת	shlo_shim_ ve-a_KHat_
40	ארבעים	arba'im
50	חמישים	KHami_shim_
60	שישים	shi_shim_
70	שבעים	shiv'_im_
80	שמונים	shmo_nim_
90	תשעים	tish'_im_
100	מאה	me'_a_
110	מאה ועשר	me'_a_ ve-'eser
200	מאתיים	ma_tayim_
300	שלוש מאות	shlosh me'_ot_
400	ארבע מאות	ar_ba_ me'_ot_
500	חמש מאות	KHa_mesh_ me'_ot_
600	שש מאות	shesh me'_ot_
700	שבע מאות	shva me'_ot_
800	שמונה מאות	shmo_neh_ me'_ot_
900	תשע מאות	te_sha_ me'_ot_
1,000	אלף	_elef_
10,000	עשרת אלפים	_as_eret ala_fim_
20,000	עשרים אלף	es_rim elef_
100,000	מאה אלף	me'_a_ _elef_
1,000,000	מיליון	mili_on_

TIME

today	היום	*ha<u>yom</u>*
yesterday	אתמול	*et<u>mol</u>*
tomorrow	מחר	*ma<u>KHar</u>*
the day before yesterday	שלשום	*shil<u>shom</u>*
the day after tomorrow	מחרתיים	*moKHro<u>tay</u>im*
this week	השבוע	*ha-sha<u>vu</u>'a*
last week	השבוע שעבר	*ha-sha<u>vu</u>'a she-'a<u>var</u>*
next week	השבוע הבא	*ha-sha<u>vu</u>'a ha-<u>ba</u>*
this morning	הבוקר	*ha-<u>bo</u>ker*
this afternoon	אחר הצהריים	*a<u>KHar</u> ha-tzoho<u>ray</u>im*
this evening	הערב	*ha-<u>e</u>rev*
tonight	הלילה	*ha-<u>lai</u>la*
yesterday afternoon	אתמול אחר הצהריים	*et<u>mol</u> a<u>KHar</u> ha-tzoho<u>ray</u>im*
last night	אמש	*<u>e</u>mesh*
tomorrow morning	מחר בבוקר	*ma<u>KHar</u> ba-<u>bo</u>ker*
tomorrow evening	מחר בערב	*ma<u>KHar</u> ba-<u>e</u>rev*
in three days	עוד שלושה ימים	*od shlo<u>sha</u> ya<u>mim</u>*
three days ago	לפני שלושה ימים	*lif<u>nay</u> shlo<u>sha</u> ya<u>mim</u>*
late	מאוחר	*me'u<u>KHar</u>*
early	מוקדם	*muk<u>dam</u>*
soon	בקרוב	*beka<u>rov</u>*
later on	אחר כך	*a<u>KHar</u> kaKH*
at the moment	כרגע	*ka<u>re</u>ga*

second	שניה	shni<u>ya</u>
minute	דקה	da<u>ka</u>
one minute	דקה אחת	da<u>ka</u> a<u>KH</u>at
two minutes	שתי דקות	shtay da<u>kot</u>
quarter of an hour	רבע שעה	<u>reva</u> sha'a
half an hour	חצי שעה	<u>KHatzi</u> sha'a
forty-five minutes	שלושת רבעי שעה	shloshet riv'<u>ay</u> sha'a
hour	שעה	sha'a
that day	אותו היום	oto ha-<u>yom</u>
every day	כל יום	kol yom
all day	כל היום	kol ha-<u>yom</u>
the next day	למחרת	lemo<u>KHorat</u>

TELLING TIME

"It's . . . o'clock" in Hebrew is **ha-sha'a** . . ., followed by the number of the hour. "It's two o'clock" is, therefore, **ha-sha'a <u>shtayim</u>**. "Quarter past" is **va-<u>reva</u>**, so "quarter past two" is **<u>shtayim</u> va-<u>reva</u>**. "Half past" is **va-<u>KHetzi</u>**, so "half past two" is **<u>shtayim</u> va-<u>KHetzi</u>**. "Quarter to" is **<u>reva</u>** so "quarter to three" is **<u>reva</u> le-sha<u>losh</u>**. Any number of minutes after two o'clock would be **<u>shtayim</u> ve-. . . da<u>kot</u>**. Any number of minutes (if it is less than thirty) before three o'clock would be . . . **da<u>kot</u> le-sha<u>losh</u>**. The twenty-four hour clock is used solely for military purposes. To distinguish between AM and PM, it's possible to use the words "in the morning" **ba-<u>boker</u>**, "in the afternoon" **a<u>KH</u>a<u>ray</u> ha-tzoho<u>ray</u>im**, "in the evening" **ba-<u>erev</u>**, or "at night" **ba-<u>laila</u>**. Thus, "7 AM" would be **<u>sheva</u> ba-<u>boker</u>**, and "4 PM"—**<u>arba</u> a<u>KH</u>a<u>ray</u> ha-tzoho<u>ray</u>im**.

AM	בבוקר	ba-_boker_
PM (afternoon)	בצהריים, אחרי הצהריים	ba-tzoho_rayim_, aKHa_ray_ ha-tzoho_rayim_
(evening)	בערב	ba-_erev_
one o'clock	אחת	a_KHat_
ten past one	אחת ועשרה	a_KHat_ va-'asa_ra_
quarter past one	אחת ורבע	a_KHat_ va-_reva_
half past one	אחת וחצי	a_KHat_ va-_KHetzi_
twenty to two	עשרים לשתיים	esrim le-_shtayim_
quarter to two	רבע לשתיים	_reva_ le-_shtayim_
two o'clock	שתיים	_shtayim_
13:00	אחת	a_KHat_
16:30	ארבע וחצי	_arba_ va-_KHetzi_
at half past five	בחמש וחצי	be-_KHamesh_ va-_KHetzi_
at seven o'clock	בשבע	be-_sheva_
noon	שתים עשרה בצהריים	_shtaym esreh_ ba-tzoho_rayim_
midnight	חצות	KHa_tzot_

HOTELS

Israel's hotels are ranked by the Ministry of Tourism on a scale of one to five stars, and the tourist and business traveler will have little difficulty in finding suitable accommodation. High-quality hotels are located in all the large cities such as Tel Aviv, Jerusalem, Haifa, and Eilat. It is, however, vital to make reservations well in advance during the holiday seasons (Rosh Hashana, Christmas, Easter, and Passover—see Cross-Cultural Notes, p.10–11). Seaside resorts such as Eilat, Netanya, and Nahariya have a wide variety of less expensive accommodations close to the beaches and often cater to tour groups. There is a wide range of youth hostels located throughout the country and kibbutz guesthouses **bayt ha'araKHa** (בית האראחה) or **leena kafrit** (לינה כפרית) can make an interesting alternative to hotels. Kibbutzim, communal agricultural settlements, are unique to Israel, and a visit to one is a must on any tour of the country.

   Christian hostels, situated primarily in the eastern section of Jerusalem, are similar to youth hostels but welcome all travelers. Most hotels in the Jewish areas of Israel keep kosher (the dietary laws prescribed in Judaism—see Cross-Cultural Notes, p.9) and observe the Sabbath. For the tourist, this will mean that Friday night and Saturday meals must be reserved in advance and that banking facilities, stores, and other services will not be available until sunset on Saturday night. Prices are normally advertised in each hotel or are available from tourist information centers.

Useful Words and Phrases

balcony	מירפסת	mirpeset
bathroom	חדר אמבטיה	KHadar ambatia
bed	מיטה	mita
bedroom	חדר שינה	KHadar shayna
bill	חשבון	KHeshbon

breakfast	ארוחת בוקר	aru_khat_ _bo_ker
dining room	חדר אוכל	_kha_dar _o_khel
dinner	ארוחת ערב	aru_khat_ _e_rev
double room	חדר זוגי	_khe_der zu_gi_
elevator	מעלית	ma'a_lit_
full board	פנסיון מלא	_pension_ ma_leh_
half board	חצי פנסיון	_kha_t_zi_ _pension_
hostel	אכסניה	a_khs_ani_ya_
hotel	מלון	ma_lon_
key	מפתח	maf_te_a_kh_
kibbutz guesthouse	בית הארחה	bayt ha'ara_kha_
lobby	לובי	_lo_bi
lounge	אולם	u_lam_
lunch	ארוחת צהריים	aru_khat_ _tzoho_ra_yim
manager (_male_)	מנהל	mena_hel_
(_female_)	מנהלת	mena_hel_et
reception	קבלה	kaba_la_
receptionist (_male_)	פקיד קבלה	pkid kaba_la_
(_female_)	פקידת קבלה	pki_dat_ kaba_la_
restaurant	מסעדה	mis'a_da_
room	חדר	_khe_der
room service	שירות חדרים	she_rut_ _kha_da_rim_
shower	מיקלחת	mik_la_khat
single room	חדר ליחיד	_khe_der le-ya_khid_
toilet/restroom	שירותים	sheru_tim_
twin room	חדר זוגי עם מיטות נפרדות	_khe_der zu_gi_ im mi_tot_ nifra_dot_

Have you any vacancies?

יש לכם חדרים פנויים?

yesh laKHem KHadar<u>im</u> pnuy<u>im</u>?

I have a reservation

יש לי הזמנה לחדר

yesh li hazman<u>a</u> le-KHeder

I'd like a single/double room

אבקש חדר ליחיד/זוגי

avak<u>esh</u> KHeder le-yaKHid/zugi

I'd like a twin room

אבקש חדר זוגי עם מיטות נפרדות

avak<u>esh</u> KHeder zug<u>i</u> im mi<u>tot</u> nifra<u>dot</u>

I'd like a room with a bathroom/balcony

אבקש חדר עם אמבטיה/מירפסת

avak<u>esh</u> KHeder im amb<u>a</u>tia/mirp<u>e</u>set

I'd like a room for one night/three nights

אבקש חדר ללילה אחד/לשלושה לילות

avak<u>esh</u> KHeder le-<u>lai</u>la eKHad/lishlosha layl<u>ot</u>

What is the charge per night?

מה המחיר ללילה?

ma ha-meKHir le-<u>lai</u>la?

I don't know yet how long I'll stay

עוד לא ידוע לי כמה זמן אשאר

od lo yad<u>u</u>'a li <u>ka</u>ma zman esha'<u>er</u>

When is breakfast/dinner?

מתי ארוחת הבוקר/הערב?

matai aruKHAT ha-boker/ha-'erev?

Would you have my baggage brought up?

אפשר בבקשה להעלות את המיזוודות שלי?

efshar bevakasha leha'alot et ha-mizvadot sheli?

Please call me at . . . o'clock

בבקשה לצלצל אלי בשעה ...

bevakasha letzaltzel elai besha'a . . .

May I have breakfast in my room?

אפשר לקבל ארוחת בוקר לחדר?

efshar lekabel aruKHAT boker laKHeder?

I'll be back at . . . o'clock

אחזור בשעה ...

eKHezor besha'a . . .

My room number is . . .

מספר החדר שלי הוא ...

mispar haKHeder sheli hu . . .

I'm leaving tomorrow

אני עוזב/עוזבת מחר

ani ozev (m)/ozevet (f) maKHar

THINGS YOU'LL SEE

ארוחת בוקר	aru<u>KH</u>at <u>bo</u>ker	breakfast
מים עמוקים	ma<u>yim</u> amu<u>kim</u>	deep water
חדר אוכל	<u>KH</u>a<u>dar</u> <u>o</u>KHel	dining room
ארוחת ערב	aru<u>KH</u>at <u>e</u>rev	dinner
מעלית	ma'a<u>lit</u>	elevator
יציאת חירום	yetzi'<u>at</u> <u>KH</u>e<u>rum</u>	emergency exit
כניסה	kni<u>sa</u>	entrance
יציאה	yetzi'<u>a</u>	exit
ארוחת צהריים	aru<u>KH</u>at tzoho<u>ra</u>yim	lunch
הנהלה	hanha<u>la</u>	management
מנהל	mena<u>hel</u>	manager
גברים	gva<u>rim</u>	men's restroom
תפריט	ta<u>frit</u>	menu
אין כניסה	ayn kni<u>sa</u>	no entry
אין יציאה	ayn yetzi'<u>a</u>	no exit
נא לנקות את החדר	na lena<u>kot</u> et ha-<u>KH</u>eder	please clean the room
נא לא להפריע	na lo lehafri'<u>a</u>	please do not disturb
נא לא לעשן	na lo le'a<u>shen</u>	please do not smoke
קבלה	kaba<u>la</u>	reception
שירותים	sheru<u>tim</u>	restroom
מים רדודים	ma<u>yim</u> redu<u>dim</u>	shallow water
חדר טלויזיה	<u>KH</u>adar tele<u>vi</u>zia	television room
לבריכת השחייה	le-bray<u>KH</u>at ha-s<u>KH</u>iya	to the swimming pool
נשים	na<u>shim</u>	women's restroom

THINGS YOU'LL HEAR

slikHa, anakHnu mele'im
I'm sorry, we're full

lo nish'aru KHadarim le-yaKHid
There are no single rooms left

lo nish'aru KHadarim zugiyim
There are no double rooms left

le-kama laylot?
For how many nights?

ma shimKHa (*to a man*)/ma shmeKH (*to a woman*)?
What is your name?

eKH ata meshalem (*to a man*)/eKH at meshalemet (*to a woman*)?
How will you be paying?

bevakasha leshalem me-rosh
Please pay in advance

efshar lir'ot et ha-darkon bevakasha?
May I see your passport, please?

CAMPING

Israel offers much in the way of outdoor activities, such as hiking and camping. There's a nationwide system of nature reserves and marked paths as well as standard campsites. Before setting out, however, it is imperative to check with a local tourist office or with the nature preservation authorities about camping permission, security regulations, and weather conditions.

Due to the country's small size and closed borders, campers are not a practical way of traveling. Israel has an extensive system of good youth hostels, some of which are affiliated with the Youth Hostel Association, while others are private. Advance booking is recommended during holiday periods and in the summer months.

Hitchhiking is a common practice, but not a safe one. Men and women alone, and even two women together, are strongly advised not to hitchhike and to use the extensive bus service instead.

USEFUL WORDS AND PHRASES

backpack	תרמיל גב	tarmil gav
campfire	מדורה	medura
campsite	(אתר) קמפינג	(atar) kemping
cooking utensils	כלי בישול	klay bishul
drinking water	מי שתיה	may shtiya
faucet	ברז	berez
garbage	אשפה	ashpa
hitchhike	לקחת טרמפים	lakaкнat trempim
hitchhiking	טרמפ	tremp
kitchen	מטבח	mitbaкн
restrooms	שירותים	shayrutim
rope	חבל	кнevel

33

saucepans	סירים	si*rim*
showers	מקלחות	miklaKHot
sink	כיור	ki*yor*
sleeping bag	שק שינה	sak shay*na*
tent	אוהל	*ohel*
tourist office	מודיעין	modi'*in*
youth hostel	אכסניית נוער	aKHsan*yat* no'*ar*

Can I camp here?

אפשר להקים כאן אוהל?

efshar leha*kim* kan *ohel*?

Where is the nearest campsite?

איפה יש בסביבה אתר קמפינג?

ayfo yesh ba-svi*va* *atar* *kem*ping?

What is the charge per night?

כמה זה עולה ללילה?

kama zeh o*leh* le-*lai*la?

Can I light a fire here?

אפשר להדליק כאן מדורה?

efshar lehad*lik* kan medu*ra*?

Where can I get . . .?

איפה אפשר להשיג ...?

ayfo ef*shar* leha*sig* . . .?

Is there drinking water here?
יש כאן מי שתיה?
yesh kan may shtiya?

THINGS YOU'LL SEE OR HEAR

קמפינג	<u>kemping</u>	campsite
תשלום, תעריף	ta'<u>arif</u>, tash<u>lum</u>	charges
שטח סגור	<u>she</u>taкн sagur	closed area
זהירות!	zehi<u>rut</u>!	danger!
מי שתיה	may shtiya	drinking water
אש	esh	fire
שביל	shvil	footpath
להשכרה	lehaska<u>ra</u>	for rent
מטבח	mit<u>baкн</u>	kitchen
להשאיל	lehash'<u>il</u>	to lend
אור	or	light
תעודת חבר	te'u<u>dat</u> кнa<u>ver</u>	membership card
שטח צבאי	<u>she</u>taкн tzva'<u>i</u>	military area
שמורת טבע	shmu<u>rat</u> <u>te</u>va	nature preserve
לא להדליק אש	lo lehad<u>lik</u> esh	no campfires
אין כניסה	ayn kni<u>sa</u>	no entry
שירותים	shayru<u>tim</u>	restrooms
מקלחת	mik<u>laкн</u>at	shower
אכסניית נוער	aкнsan<u>yat</u> <u>no</u>'ar	youth hostel

DRIVING

In Israel you drive on the right and pass on the left. There are several highways, the main ones being Tel Aviv-Jerusalem and Tel Aviv-Haifa. There are no traffic circles. All secondary roads give way to main roads at junctions and intersections, but in the case of roads or junctions not marked, the traffic coming from the RIGHT has priority.

The overall quality of roads is adequate, although minor roads are often bumpy and have dangerous curves. Parking is a problem in Tel Aviv, and you'll see many cars parked on sidewalks. Rush hour in the large cities is approximately between 7:30 and 9:00 AM. The evening rush hour varies but tends to peak at around 5 PM. Routes to Tel Aviv may become very busy on Saturday evenings too.

Distances and speed are always measured in kilometers. The speed limit on highways is 90 km/h (55 mph), on other inter-city roads 80 km/h (50 mph), and in built-up areas 50 km/h (30 mph). Seat belts must be worn in the front seats at all times; seat belts in the back are compulsory for children up to the age of four.

Many gas stations are open twenty-four hours a day. Fuel ratings are as follows: 91 octane/super unleaded ok<u>t</u>an tish'im ve-'a<u>kh</u>at (91 אוקטן), 96 octane/premium ok<u>t</u>an tish'im ve-<u>shesh</u> (96 אוקטן) diesel <u>d</u>izel (דיזל), and unleaded gas ne<u>t</u>ul o<u>f</u>eret (נטול עופרת).

Israeli drivers can be aggressive and are seldom courteous; accident rates are, unfortunately, high. Be on the lookout for dangerous drivers, and don't take your right of way for granted!

SOME COMMON ROAD SIGNS

זהירות	zehirut	caution
ילדים חוצים את הכביש	yeladim KHotzim et ha-kvish	children crossing
סכנה	sakana	danger
עקומה חדה	akuma KHada	dangerous curve
צומת מסוכן	tzomet mesukan	dangerous junction
עזרה ראשונה	ezra rishona	first aid
רכב כבד	reKHev kaved	for heavy vehicles
מוסך	musaKH	garage
דלק	delek	gas
תחנת דלק	taKHanat delek	gas station
כבה אורות	kabeh orot	headlights off
הדלק אורות	hadlek orot	headlights on
כביש מהיר	kvish mahir	highway
הצטלבות	hitztalvut	intersection
צומת	tzomet	junction
איזור אש	ezor esh	military training area
גשר צר	gesher tzar	narrow bridge
כביש צר	kvish tzar	narrow road
אין כניסה	ayn knisa	no entry
אין חניה	ayn KHanaya	no parking
אין עקיפה	ayn akifa	no passing
כביש חד סטרי	kvish KHad sitri	one-way street
חניה	KHanaya	parking
חניון	KHenyon	parking lot

→

מדרחוב	midreкноv	pedestrian area
מעבר חציה	ma'avar кнatziya	pedestrian crossing
הולכי רגל	holкнay regel	pedestrians
עבודות בכביש	avodot ba-kvish	roadwork
בית ספר	bayt sefer	school
רוח צד	ruaкн tzad	side wind
האט	ha'et	slow
עצור	atzor	stop
מרכז העיר	merkaz ha-'ir	town center
מעבר תת קרקעי	ma'avar tat karka'i	underground passage
תן זכות קדימה	ten zкнut kdima	yield

USEFUL WORDS AND PHRASES

automatic (*noun*)	אוטומטי	otomati
brake (*noun*)	מעצור	ma'atzor
breakdown	תקלה	takala
camper (*van*)	קרוון	karavan
car	מכונית	meкнonit
clutch	קלץ'	klach
to drive	לנהוג	linhog
engine	מנוע	mano'a
exhaust	אגזוז	egzoz
fan belt	רצועת מאוורר	retzu'at me'avrer
garage (*for repairs*)	מוסך	musaкн
gas	דלק	delek
gas station	תחנת דלק	taкнanat delek
gear	מהלך, הילוך	mahalaкн, hiluкн

headlights	אורות קדמיים	_orot_ kidmi_yim_
highway	כביש מהיר	kvish ma_hir_
intersection	הצטלבות	hitztal_vut_
junction (_on highway_)	צומת, מחלף	_tzomet_, meK_Hlaf_
kilometer	קילומטר	kilo_meter_
license	רשיון	risha_yon_
license plate	לוחית זיהוי	luK_Hit_ zi_hui_
manual gears	תיבת הילוכים ידנית	tay_yat_ hiluK_Him_ yada_nit_
mirror	ראי	re_i_
motorcycle	אופנוע	ofa_no_'a
road	כביש	kvish
spare parts	חלקי חילוף	K_Hel_ka_y_ K_Hi_luf_
speed (_noun_)	מהירות	mehi_rut_
speed limit	מהירות מותרת	mehi_rut_ mu_teret_
speedometer	ספידומטר	spido_meter_
steering wheel	הגה	_hegeh_
street	רחוב	reK_HOV_
taillights	אורות אחוריים	_orot_ aK_Hori_yim_
tire	צמיג	tza_mig_
to tow	לגרור	lig_ror_
traffic lights	רמזור	ramz_or_
truck	משאית	masa_'it_
trunk	תא מיטען	ta mit_'an_
van	רכב מסחרי	re_Khev_ misK_Ha_ri_
wheel	גלגל	gal_gal_
windshield	שימשה קדמית	shim_sha_ kid_mit_
windshield wiper	וישר	_visher_

I'd like some gas/oil/water

דלק / שמן / מים, בבקשה

<u>de</u>lek/<u>she</u>men/<u>ma</u>yim, bevaka<u>sha</u>

Fill her up, please!

מלא, בבקשה!

ma<u>leh</u>, bevaka<u>sha</u>!

I'd like ten liters of gas

עשרה ליטר דלק, בבקשה

asa<u>ra</u> <u>li</u>ter <u>de</u>lek, bevaka<u>sha</u>

Would you check the tires, please?

אפשר לבדוק את הצמיגים, בבקשה?

ef<u>shar</u> liv<u>dok</u> et ha-tzmi<u>gim</u>, bevaka<u>sha</u>?

Do you do repairs?

אתם עושים תיקונים?

a<u>tem</u> o<u>sim</u> tiku<u>nim</u>?

Can you repair the clutch?

אפשר לתקן את הקלץ'?

ef<u>shar</u> leta<u>ken</u> et ha-<u>klach</u>?

How long will it take?

כמה זמן זה יקח?

<u>ka</u>ma zman zeh yi<u>kaкн</u>?

Where can I park?

איפה אפשר לחנות?

<u>ay</u>fo ef<u>shar</u> laкн<u>not</u>?

There is something wrong with the engine
יש בעייה במנוע
yesh be'aya ba-mano'a

The engine is overheating
המנוע מתחמם
ha-mano'a mitкнamem

I need a new tire
צריך צמיג חדש
ani tzariкн tzamig кнadash

I'd like to rent a car
אבקש לשכור מכונית
avakesh liskor meкнonit

Is there a mileage charge?
יש חיוב נוסף לפי קילומטרים?
yesh кнiyuv nosaf lefi kilometrim?

Where is the nearest garage?
איפה המוסך הקרוב ביותר?
ayfo ha-musaкн ha-karov bayoter?

How do I get to . . .?
איך מגיעים ל...?
ayкн magi'im le-. . .?

Is this the road to . . .?
זאת הדרך ל...?
zot ha-dereкн le-. . .?

DIRECTIONS YOU MAY BE GIVEN

<u>ya</u>shar	straight ahead
mi<u>smol</u>	on the left
<u>smo</u>la	turn left
mi<u>ya</u>min	on the right
ya<u>mi</u>na	turn right
ri<u>shon</u> mi<u>ya</u>min	first on the right
<u>she</u>ni mi<u>smol</u>	second on the left
aкн<u>aray</u> ha-. . .	past the . . .

THINGS YOU'LL SEE

לחץ אויר	<u>la</u>кнatz <u>a</u>vir	air pressure
דיזל	<u>di</u>zel	diesel
יציאה	yetzi<u>'a</u>	exit
דלק	<u>de</u>lek	gas
תחנת דלק	taкн<u>a</u>nat <u>de</u>lek	gas station
כביש מהיר	kvish ma<u>hir</u>	highway
צומת, מחלף	<u>tzo</u>met, meкн<u>laf</u>	highway junction
שמן	<u>she</u>men	oil
גובה שמן	<u>go</u>va <u>she</u>men	oil level
אוקטן 96	ok<u>tan</u> tish<u>'im</u> ve-<u>shesh</u>	premium grade
תיקון	ti<u>kun</u>	repair
נתיב איטי	na<u>tiv</u> <u>i</u>ti	slow lane
אוקטן 91	ok<u>tan</u> tish<u>'im</u> ve-aкн<u>at</u>	super unleaded grade
לחץ צמיגים	<u>la</u>кнatz tzmi<u>gim</u>	tire pressure
פקק תנועה	pkak tnu<u>'a</u>	traffic jam
נטול עופרת	ne<u>tul</u> o<u>fe</u>ret	unleaded

THINGS YOU'LL HEAR

otomati o yadani?
Would you like an automatic or a manual?

rishayon, bevakasha
May I see your license?

TRAIN TRAVEL

Israel's train system is limited and far surpassed by the efficient bus system (see By Bus and Taxi, p.55). Most trains are old, facilities simple, and distances relatively short. The best service runs from Tel Aviv to Haifa, via Netanya; it is regular and fast enough to offer a real alternative to road travel. The train ride from Tel Aviv up to Jerusalem is slow, but it is well worth making as a leisure trip for the beautiful scenery. A new urban railroad system is currently being planned for Tel Aviv and its metropolitan area.

USEFUL WORDS AND PHRASES

baggage cart	עגלת מטען	eglat mit'an
baggage room	שמירת חפצים	shmirat KHafatzim
buffet	מזנון	miznon
car (of a train)	קרון	karon
engine	קטר	katar
entrance	כניסה	knisa
exit	יציאה	yetzi'a
first class	מחלקה ראשונה	maKHlaka rishona
to get in	להיכנס	lehikanes
to get out	לצאת	latzet
lost and found	אבידות	avaydot
one-way ticket	כרטיס בכיוון אחד	kartis beKHivun eKHad
platform	רציף	ratzif
railroad	רכבת	rakevet
reservation office	משרד כרטיסים	misrad kartisim
reserved seat	מקום שמור	makom shamur
restaurant car	קרון מסעדה	kron mis'ada

round trip ticket	כרטיס הלוך ושוב	*kartis* haloкн va*shov*
seat	מושב	*moshav*
second class	מחלקה שניה	maкнla*ka* shni*ya*
station	תחנה	taкнa*na*
ticket	כרטיס	*kartis*
ticket inspector	מבקר כרטיסים	meva*ker* karti*sim*
timetable	לוח זמנים	*lu*aкн zma*nim*
train	רכבת	*rakevet*
waiting room	חדר המתנה	кнa*dar* hamtana
window	חלון	кнa*lon*

When does the train for . . . leave?
מתי יוצאת הרכבת ל...?
matai yotzet ha-rakevet le-. . .?

When is the next train to . . .?
מתי הרכבת הבאה ל...?
matai ha-rakevet ha-ba'a le-. . .?

When is the first train to . . .?
מתי הרכבת הראשונה ל...?
matai ha-rakevet ha-rishona le-. . .?

When is the last train to . . .?
מתי הרכבת האחרונה ל...?
matai ha-rakevet ha-aкнrona le-. . .?

What is the fare to . . .?
כמה עולה כרטיס ל...?
kama oleh kartis le-. . .?

Does the train stop at . . .?

הרכבת עוצרת ב...?

ha-ra<u>ke</u>vet ot<u>ze</u>ret be-. . .?

How long does it take to get to . . .?

כמה זמן הנסיעה ל...?

<u>ka</u>ma zman ha-nesi<u>‘a</u> le-. . .?

A one-way/round trip ticket to . . ., please

כרטיס בכיוון אחד/הלוך ושוב ל..., בבקשה

kar<u>tis</u> beKHi<u>vun</u> eKHad/haloKH va-<u>shov</u> le-. . ., bevaka<u>sha</u>

I'd like to reserve a seat

אבקש מקום שמור

ava<u>kesh</u> ma<u>kom</u> sha<u>mur</u>

Is this the right train for . . .?

זו הרכבת ל...?

zo ha-ra<u>ke</u>vet le-. . .?

Is the train late?

הרכבת מאחרת?

ha-ra<u>ke</u>vet me‘aKH<u>e</u>ret?

Could you help me with my baggage, please?

אפשר לקבל עזרה עם המיטען, בבקשה?

ef<u>shar</u> leka<u>bel</u> ez<u>ra</u> im ha-mit<u>‘an</u>, bevaka<u>sha</u>?

Is this a nonsmoking compartment?

זה קרון ללא מעשנים?

zeh ka<u>ron</u> le<u>lo</u> me‘ash<u>nim</u>?

Is this seat free?
המושב הזה פנוי?
ha-moshav ha-zeh panui?

This seat is taken
המושב הזה תפוס
ha-moshav ha-zeh tafus

I have reserved this seat
המושב הזה שמור לי
ha-moshav ha-zeh shamur li

May I open/close the window?
אפשר לפתוח/לסגור את החלון?
efshar lifto'akh/lisgor et ha-khalon?

What station is this?
איזו תחנה זאת?
ayzo takhana zot?

Do we stop at . . .?
עוצרים ב...?
otzrim be-. . .?

THINGS YOU'LL SEE

שמירת חפצים	shmir<u>at</u> KHafa<u>tzim</u>	baggage storage
מזנון	mizno<u>n</u>	buffet
קרון	kar<u>on</u>	car *(of a train)*
עיכוב	ik<u>uv</u>	delay
מעצור חירום	ma'a<u>tzor</u> KHe<u>rum</u>	emergency brake
תפוס	taf<u>us</u>	engaged
כניסה	kni<u>sa</u>	entrance
יציאה	yetzi'<u>a</u>	exit
מידע, מודיעין	may<u>da</u> modi'<u>in</u>	information
אין כניסה	ayn kni<u>sa</u>	no entry
לא מעשנים	lo me'ash<u>nim</u>	nonsmokers
רציף	rat<u>zif</u>	platform
מעשנים	me'ash<u>nim</u>	smokers
קופה	ku<u>pa</u>	ticket office
כרטיסים	karti<u>sim</u>	tickets
לוח זמנים	lu<u>a</u>KH zma<u>nim</u>	timetable
חדר המתנה	KHa<u>dar</u> hamta<u>na</u>	waiting room

THINGS YOU'LL HEAR

zehi<u>rut</u>
Attention, be careful

karti<u>sim</u>, bevaka<u>sha</u>
Tickets, please

AIR TRAVEL

Israel's main international airport is Ben-Gurion Airport, fifteen
minutes drive to Tel Aviv and forty minutes to Jerusalem. Some
international flights land in Eilat, and the domestic
connections include smaller airports in northern Tel Aviv,
Jerusalem, and the northern part of the country. However,
Israel's size means that all destinations are within easy driving
distance. Travelers planning to go to Arab countries, with the
exception of Egypt, may do well to request that their passport
not be stamped by Israeli passport control.

USEFUL WORDS AND PHRASES

aircraft	מטוס	*matos*
airline	חברת תעופה	*KHevrat te'ufa*
airport	שדה תעופה	*sdeh te'ufa*
airport shuttle	אוטובוס שדה תעופה	*otobus sdeh te'ufa*
aisle seat	מושב ליד המעבר	*moshav leyad ha-ma'avar*
arrivals	טיסות נכנסות	*tisot niKHnasot*
baggage claim	מיטען	*mit'an*
boarding pass	כרטיס עליה למטוס	*kartis aliya la-matos*
check-in	צ׳ק אין	*chek in*
check-in desk	דלפק קבלת נוסעים	*dalpak kabalat nos'im*
customs	מכס	*meKHes*
delay	עיכוב	*ikuv*
departure	טיסות יוצאות	*tisot yotz'ot*
departure lounge	אולם נוסעים יוצאים	*ulam nos'im yotz'im*
emergency exit	יציאת חירום	*yetzi'at KHerum*
flight	טיסה	*tisa*

49

flight attendant (*female*)	דיילת	*dayelet*
flight attendant (*male*)	דייל	*dayal*
flight number	מיספר טיסה	*mispar tisa*
gate	שער	*sha'ar*
jet	סילון	*silon*
land (*verb*)	לנחות	*linKHot*
long distance flight	טיסה ארוכה	*tisa aruka*
passport	דרכון	*darkon*
passport control	ביקורת דרכונים	*bikoret darkonim*
pilot	טייס	*tayas*
runway	מסלול	*maslul*
seat	מושב	*moshav*
seat belt	חגורת בטיחות	*KHagorat betiKHut*
takeoff	המראה	*hamra'a*
window	חלון	*KHalon*
wing	כנף	*kanaf*

When is there a flight to . . .?
?...מתי יש טיסה ל
matai yesh tisa le-. . .?

What time does the flight to . . . leave?
?...מתי יוצאת הטיסה ל
matai yotzet ha-tisa le-. . .?

Is it a direct flight?
?זאת טיסה ישירה
zot tisa yeshira?

Do I have to change planes?
צריך להחליף מטוס?
tzariкн lehaкнlif ma<u>tos</u>?

When do I have to check in?
מתי צריך להגיע לטיסה?
ma<u>tai</u> tzariкн lehagi'a la-<u>tisa</u>?

I'd like a one-way ticket to . . .
אבקש כרטיס טיסה בכיוון אחד ל...
ava<u>kesh</u> kar<u>tis</u> <u>tisa</u> be-кнi<u>vun</u> eкнad le-. . .

I'd like a round trip ticket to . . .
אבקש כרטיס טיסה הלוך ושוב ל...
ava<u>kesh</u> kar<u>tis</u> <u>tisa</u> haloкн va-<u>shov</u> le-. . .

I'd like a nonsmoking seat, please
לא מעשנים, בבקשה
<u>lo</u> me'ash<u>nim</u>, bevaka<u>sha</u>

I'd like a window seat, please
ליד החלון, בבקשה
le<u>yad</u> ha-кнa<u>lon</u>, bevaka<u>sha</u>

How long will the flight be delayed?
כמה זמן הטיסה מתעכבת?
<u>kama</u> zman ha-<u>tisa</u> mit'a<u>kevet</u>?

Is this the right gate for the . . . flight?
זה השער הנכון לטיסה ל...?
zeh ha-<u>sha</u>'ar ha-naкнon la-<u>tisa</u> le-. . .?

AIR TRAVEL

Which gate for the flight to . . .?
?...איזה שער לטיסה ל
ayzeh sha'ar la-tisa le-. . .?

When do we arrive in . . .?
?...מתי נגיע ל
matai nagi'a le-. . .?

May I smoke now?
?אפשר לעשן עכשיו
efshar le'ashen aкнshav?

I do not feel very well
אני לא מרגיש/מרגישה טוב
ani lo margish (m)/margisha (f) tov

Please don't stamp my passport
בבקשה לא להחתים את הדרכון שלי
bevakasha lo lehaкнtim et ha-darkon sheli

THINGS YOU'LL SEE

מטוס	**matos**	aircraft
גובה	**gova**	altitude
טיסות נכנסות	**tisot niкнnasot**	arrivals
מיטען	**mit'an**	baggage claim
טיסת צ'ארטר	**tisat charter**	charter flight
ביקורת מכס	**bikoret meкнes**	customs
עיכוב	**ikuv**	delay →

טיסות יוצאות	tisot yotz'ot	departures
טיסה ישירה	tisa yeshira	direct flight
טיסת פנים	tisat pnim	domestic flight
יציאת חירום	yetzi'at кнerum	emergency exit
נחיתת חירום	neкнitat кнerum	emergency landing
נא להדק חגורות	na lehadek кнagorot	fasten seat belt
טיסה	tisa	flight
דייל	dayal	flight attendant (male)
דיילת	dayelet	flight attendant (female)
שער	sha'ar	gate
מידע, מודיעין	mayda, modi'in	information
נחיתת ביניים	neкнitat baynayim	intermediate stop
טיסה בינלאומית	tisa baynle'umit	international flight
נחיתה	neкнita	landing
זמן מקומי	zman mekomi	local time
לא מעשנים	lo me'ashnim	nonsmokers
לא לעשן	lo le'ashen	no smoking, please
נוסעים	nos'im	passengers
דרכון	darkon	passport
ביקורת דרכונים	bikoret darkonim	passport control
טיסה סדירה	tisa sdira	scheduled flight
המראה	hamra'a	takeoff

THINGS YOU'LL HEAR

ha-nos'im be-tisa . . . mitbakshim lageshet le-sha'ar . . .
The flight for . . . is now boarding at gate . . .

zohi kri'a акнrona le-tisa . . .
This is the last call for flight . . .

BY BUS AND TAXI

Bus travel is perhaps the least expensive and most efficient way to get around in Israel. Cities and towns are linked together by a regular, frequent, and usually air-conditioned bus service that runs from dawn until midnight from Sunday to Thursday. Generally, buses stop running on Friday afternoons because of the Sabbath and services are resumed on Saturday night, although on Saturday a limited bus service now operates in Tel Aviv, Haifa, and Eilat. Inter-city tickets are purchased at the bus station and, while during the week there's usually no line, on Friday afternoons and Sunday mornings you might find yourself among crowds of soldiers and civilians going to or returning from relatives. There are discounts on inter-city tickets for senior citizens, students, and children. The bus services within the cities are also fast and efficient and you can purchase your ticket from the driver or conductor. There is a multiple-trip ticket, **kartisiya** (כרטיסיה), which can also be purchased from the driver and which can save you money if you're traveling around a lot. Discounts on these tickets are available for senior citizens and children. A monthly bus pass, **кнodshi кнofshi** (חודשי חופשי), allowing unlimited travel in Tel Aviv, is also available.

Sometimes to avoid the jostling crowd the traveler may prefer to take a taxi. There are two types of taxi travel. One is just as in the West, where it's possible to book a taxi by phone or flag one down in the street. Most have meters, but if they don't, it is essential that you agree in advance on the fare. The other type of taxi, called the **sherut** (שירות), is available for travel between the larger cities such as Tel Aviv, Jerusalem, Haifa, and Beer Sheva, and to and from the airport. These taxis are shared among about seven passengers and have a fixed route and price. The taxi and the **sherut** are also available to rent on Friday nights and Saturdays at a slightly increased fare. Tipping the taxi driver is not customary in Israel.

USEFUL WORDS AND PHRASES

adult	מבוגר	mevu<u>gar</u>
bus	אוטובוס	<u>o</u>tobus
bus map	מפת מסלולי אוטובוס	ma<u>pat</u> maslu<u>lay</u> <u>o</u>tobus
bus stop	תחנת אוטובוס	ta<u>kHa</u>nat <u>o</u>tobus
child	ילד	<u>ye</u>led
conductor	כרטיסן	karti<u>san</u>
connection	קשר	<u>ke</u>sher
driver (male)	נהג	na<u>hag</u>
(female)	נהגת	na<u>he</u>get
fare	דמי נסיעה	d<u>may</u> nesi<u>ya</u>
long-distance bus	אוטובוס	<u>o</u>tobus
main bus station	תחנה מרכזית	ta<u>kHa</u>na merka<u>zit</u>
monthly bus pass	חודשי חופשי	KHod<u>shi</u> KHof<u>shi</u>
multiple-trip ticket	כרטיסיה	kartisi<u>ya</u>
number 5 bus	אוטובוס מספר חמש	<u>o</u>tobus mis<u>par</u> KHa<u>mesh</u>
passenger (male)	נוסע	no<u>se'a</u>
(female)	נוסעת	no<u>sa'at</u>
seat	מושב	mo<u>shav</u>
taxi	מונית	mo<u>nit</u>
taxi (fixed route)	שירות	she<u>rut</u>
terminal	תחנה סופית	ta<u>kHa</u>na so<u>fit</u>
ticket	כרטיס	kar<u>tis</u>
underground passage	מעבר תת קרקעי	ma'a<u>var</u> tat karka<u>'i</u>

Where is the main bus station?

איפה התחנה המרכזית?

ayfo ha-taKHana ha-merkazit?

Where is there a bus stop?

איפה יש תחנת אוטובוס?

ayfo yesh taKHanat otobus?

Which bus goes to . . .?

איזה אוטובוס נוסע ל...?

ayzeh otobus nose'a le-. . .?

How often does the bus to . . . run?

כל כמה זמן נוסע האוטובוס ל...?

kol kama zman nose'a ha-otobus le-. . .?

Would you tell me when we get to . . .?

אפשר להגיד לי מתי מגיעים ל...?

efshar lehagid li matai magi'im le-. . .?

Do I have to get off yet?

אני צריך/צריכה לרדת?

ani tzariKH (m)/tzriKHa (f) laredet?

How do you get to . . .?

איך מגיעים ל...?

ayKH magi'im le-. . .?

Is it very far?

האם זה רחוק?

haim zeh raKHok?

I want to go to . . .

אני רוצה לנסוע ל.../אני רוצה לנסוע ל...

ani rotzeh (m)/*ani rotza* (f) *linso'a le-. . .*

Do you go near . . .?

אתה עובר על-יד ...?

ata over al-yad . . .?

Where can I buy a ticket?

איפה אפשר לקנות כרטיס?

ayfo efshar liknot kartis?

Could you open/close the window?

אפשר לפתוח/לסגור את החלון?

efshar liftoaкн/lisgor et ha-кнalon?

Could you help me get a ticket?

אפשר לעזור לי לקנות כרטיס?

efshar la'azor li liknot kartis?

Please don't push

בבקשה לא לדחוף

bevakasha lo lidкнof

When does the last bus leave?

מתי עוזב האוטובוס האחרון?

matai ozev ha-otobus ha-aкнaron?

To . . ., please

ל... בבקשה

le-. . . bevakasha

How much will it cost?

כמה זה יעלה?

kama zeh ya'aleh?

Can you wait here and take me back?

תוכל לחכות כאן ולהחזיר אותי?

tuKHal leKHakot kan ve-lehaKHzir oti?

THINGS YOU'LL SEE

מבוגרים	mevugarim	adults
מיזוג אוויר	mizug avir	air-conditioning
שים לב לחפץ חשוד!	sim lev le-KHefetz KHashud	beware of suspicious objects
להחליף	lehaKHlif	to change
ילדים	yeladim	children
נסיעה	nesi'a	departure, trip
נא לא להפריע לנהג	na lo lehafri'a la-nahag	do not disturb the driver
יציאת חירום	yetzi'at KHerum	emergency exit
כניסה	knisa	entrance
כניסה מלפנים/מאחור	knisa milfanim/mi-aKHor	entry at the front/rear
יציאה	yetzi'a	exit
מלא	maleh	full
כרטיסיה	kartisiya	multiple-trip ticket
אין כניסה	ayn knisa	no entry

59

נא לא לעשן	**na lo le'ashen**	no smoking
דרך	**derekн**	road
מסלול	**maslul**	route
מושב	**moshav**	seat
עצור	**atzor**	stop
תחנת מוניות	**takнanat moniyot**	taxi stand
תחנה סופית	**takнana sofit**	terminal
כרטיס	**kartis**	ticket

RESTAURANTS

Israel offers a rich variety of gastronomic experiences. Israeli cuisine is, typically, a blend of favorite dishes from the Middle East and from Europe; a more sophisticated cuisine, with the emphasis on fish and fruit, is also available. The Israeli breakfast is often a sumptuous meal, consisting of a fresh vegetable salad, eggs, and several types of cheese, cold meats, or fish. Coffee is the most popular hot beverage. Lunch is the big hot meal of the day, while dinner, especially in private homes, is usually smaller and often vegetarian.

Israel's restaurants are similar to those in the West as far as style and variety are concerned: everything from Mexican to Chinese can be found. In larger cities, the waiters are often students; service is friendly, although not always professional. There's usually an optional service charge of between 10 –15 percent. Fixed price menus are uncommon, and most restaurants offer only a choice of à la carte dishes. A reservation is needed for the popular or upscale establishments, especially on the weekend. At the other end of the spectrum, nutritious and inexpensive food can be bought from street stands; the most typical of such dishes is **falafel** (פלאפל), fried chickpea balls served in pita bread with ground chickpea sauce ĸнumus (חומוס), salad, and pickles.

Many, though by no means all, of Israel's restaurants keep kosher, or the dietary laws (see Cross-Cultural Notes, p.9), and will close on Friday nights and all day Saturday. If you happen to be in Jerusalem or Galilee at this time, delicious Arab cuisine is to be recommended. Ask for a <u>maza</u>, and you will be given a variety of small, tasty hors d'oeuvres.

Alcoholic drinks are served in most restaurants and bars. Israel produces its own lager-style beer and wine, and imports European products. There is a good range of fruit drinks. Tap water is usually drinkable; mineral water, local and imported, is widely available.

USEFUL WORDS AND PHRASES

bar	בר	*bar*
beer	בירה	*bira*
bill	חשבון	*KHeshbon*
bottle	בקבוק	*bakbuk*
breakfast	ארוחת בוקר	*aruKHat boker*
café	בית קפה	*bayt kafeh*
cake	עוגה	*uga*
chef (*male*)	טבח	*tabaKH*
(*female*)	טבחית	*tabaKHit*
coffee	קפה	*kafeh*
cup	ספל	*sefel*
fork	מזלג	*mazleg*
glass	כוס	*kos*
knife	סכין	*sakin*
lunch	ארוחת צהריים	*aruKHat tzohorayim*
meal	ארוחה	*aruKHa*
menu	תפריט	*tafrit*
milk	חלב	*KHalav*
napkin	מפית	*mapit*
plate	צלחת	*tzalakhat*
receipt	קבלה	*kabala*
sandwich	כריך, סנדוויץ'	*kariKH, sendvich*
snack (*sandwich, etc.*)	חטיף	*KHatif*
(*a light meal*)	ארוחה קלה	*aruKHa kala*
snack bar	מזנון	*miznon*
soup	מרק	*marak*

spoon	כף	*kaf*
sugar	סוכר	*sukar*
supper	ארוחת ערב	*aruKHat erev*
table	שולחן	*shulKHan*
tea	תה	*teh*
teaspoon	כפית	*kapit*
tip	תשר, טיפ	*tip, tesher*
vegetarian (*male*)	צמחוני	*tzimKHoni*
(*female*)	צמחונית	*tzimKHonit*
waiter	מלצר	*meltzar*
waitress	מלצרית	*meltzarit*
water	מים	*mayim*
wine	יין	*yayin*
wine list	תפריט יינות	*tafrit yaynot*

A table for one, please
שולחן ליחיד, בבקשה
shulKHan le-yaKHid, bevakasha

A table for two, please
שולחן לשניים, בבקשה
shulKHan le-shnayim, bevakasha

May I see the menu?
אפשר לראות את התפריט?
efshar lir'ot et ha-tafrit?

May I see the wine list?

אפשר לראות את תפריט היינות?

efshar lir'ot et tafrit ha-yaynot?

What would you recommend?

על מה אתה ממליץ?

al ma ata mamlitz? (to a man)

על מה את ממליצה?

al ma at mamlitza? (to a woman)

I'd like . . .

אני מבקש/מבקשת ...

ani mevakesh (m)/*mevakeshet* (f) . . .

Just a cup of coffee, please

רק כוס קפה, בבקשה

rak kos kafeh, bevakasha

Excuse me!

סליחה!

sliKHa!

May we have the bill, please?

אפשר לקבל את החשבון, בבקשה?

efshar lekabel et ha-KHeshbon, bevakasha?

I only want a snack

רק משהו קל, בבקשה

rak mashehu kal, bevakasha

I didn't order this
לא הזמנתי את זה
lo hizmanti et zeh

May we have some more . . .?
?... אפשר לקבל עוד
efshar lekabel od . . .?

The meal was very good, thank you
זה היה טוב מאד, תודה רבה
zeh haya tov meod, toda raba

My compliments to the chef!
!כל הכבוד לטבח
kol hakavod la-tabaкн!

THINGS YOU'LL SEE		
סגור	**sagur**	closed
קפה	**kafeh**	coffeehouse, café
פלאפל	**falafel**	falafel
כשר	**kasher**	kosher
פתוח	**patuaкн**	open
מסעדה	**mis'ada**	restaurant
מזנון	**miznon**	snack bar
קיוסק	**kiyosk**	street stand

THINGS YOU'LL HEAR

ana<u>кн</u>nu mele'<u>im</u>
We are fully booked

be-te'a<u>von</u>!
Enjoy your meal!

ma tish<u>tu</u>?
What would you like to drink?

MENU GUIDE

(* an asterisk indicates a dish that would not be served in a kosher restaurant)

APPETIZERS, SOUPS, AND SALADS

מתאבן	meta'a<u>ben</u>	appetizer
מרק עוף	ma<u>rak</u> off	chicken soup
כבד קצוץ	ka<u>ved</u> ka<u>tzutz</u>	chopped liver
כופתאות	kufta'<u>ot</u>	dumplings, matzo balls
ביצה רוסית	bay<u>tza</u> ru<u>sit</u>	egg salad
פלאפל	fa<u>la</u>fel	falafel—fried chickpea balls in pita bread with salad and hot pepper sauce
מנה ראשונה	ma<u>na</u> ri<u>shona</u>	first course
חומוס	KHumus	hummus (chickpeas or ground chickpea paste) served with pita bread and salad
מרק עדשים	ma<u>rak</u> ada<u>shim</u>	lentil soup
חמוצים	KHamu<u>tzim</u>	pickles (cucumber, tomato, pepper, etc.)
סלט תפוחי אדמה	sa<u>lat</u> tapuKHay ada<u>ma</u>	potato salad
סלט	sa<u>lat</u>	salad
סלט חריף	sa<u>lat</u> KHa<u>rif</u>	spicy salad, usually with hot peppers
חציל ממולא	KHatzil memu<u>la</u>	stuffed eggplant
פלפל ממולא	pil<u>pel</u> memu<u>la</u>	stuffed pepper
שזיפים ממולאים	shezi<u>fim</u> memula'<u>im</u>	stuffed prunes

ממולאים	**memula'im**	stuffed vegetables or fruit
מרק	**ma<u>rak</u>**	soup
סלט ירקות	**sa<u>lat</u> yera<u>kot</u>**	vegetable salad
מרק ירקות	**ma<u>rak</u> yera<u>kot</u>**	vegetable soup

EGGS, CHEESE, AND PASTA

גבינה	**gvi<u>na</u>**	cheese
גבינת קוטג׳	**gvi<u>nat</u> kotej**	cottage cheese
גבינת שמנת	**gvi<u>nat</u> shamenet**	cream cheese (high-fat)
גבינה לבנה	**gvi<u>na</u> leva<u>na</u>**	cream cheese (low- or medium-fat)
ביצה	**bay<u>tza</u>**	egg
ביצה קשה	**bay<u>tza</u> ka<u>sha</u>**	hard-boiled egg
גבינה קשה	**gvi<u>na</u> ka<u>sha</u>**	hard cheese
גבינה צהובה	**gvi<u>na</u> tzehu<u>ba</u>**	hard, yellow, mild cheese
אטריות	**itri<u>yot</u>**	noodles
חביתה	**кHavi<u>ta</u>**	omelette
פסטה	**<u>pasta</u>**	pasta
ביצה מקושקשת	**bay<u>tza</u> mekush<u>kes</u>het**	scrambled eggs
ביצה רכה	**bay<u>tza</u> ra<u>ka</u>**	soft-boiled egg

FISH

קרפיון	**karpi<u>yon</u>**	carp
פילה	**fil<u>eh</u>**	fillet
דג	**dag**	fish
דג ממולא	**dag memu<u>la</u>**	gefilte fish— a seasoned fish ball

סלמון	**salmon**	salmon
דג מלוח	**dag maluakн**	salted herring
פירות ים	**payrot yam**	seafood*
חסילונים	**кhasilonim**	shrimp, prawns
סול	**sol**	sole
קלמרי	**kalamari**	squid*
אמנון	**amnun**	St. Peter's fish (freshwater fish from Sea of Galilee)
פורל	**forel**	trout

MEAT AND FOWL

בקר	**bakar**	beef
מוח	**moакн**	brains
חזה	**кнazeh**	breast
עוף	**off**	chicken
תרנגולת	**tarnegolet**	chicken
ברוז	**barvaz**	duck
פילה	**fileh**	fillet
גולש	**gulash**	goulash
טלה	**taleh**	lamb
רגל	**regel**	leg
כבד	**kaved**	liver
בשר	**basar**	meat
שיפוד	**shipud**	meat on a skewer
כבש	**keves**	mutton, lamb
בשר לבן	**basar lavan**	pork*
צלע	**tzela**	rib

נקניק	**naknik**	sausage (beef)
שניצל	**shnitzel**	schnitzel—slice of veal, coated in breadcrumbs and fried
אומצה, סטייק	**umtza, stayk**	steak
צלי	**tzli**	stew
לשון	**lashon**	tongue
תרנגול הודו	**tarnegol hodu**	turkey
עגל	**egel**	veal

Main Dishes

חמין	**KHamin**	cholent, a rich stew of meat, beans, and potatoes
שקשוקה	**shakshuka**	dish of fried vegetables and egg
קבב	**kabab**	lamb kabob
מנה עיקרית	**mana ikarit**	main course
קציצה	**ketzitza**	meatballs, served with rice or vegetables
שווארמה	**shawarma**	pieces of roasted lamb
סטייק לבן	**stayk lavan**	pork steak*
ששליק	**shishlik**	shish kabob—pieces of meat and vegetables grilled on a skewer
אומצה, סטייק	**umtza, stayk**	steak
בלינצ׳ס	**blinches**	thin pancakes filled with cheese or spinach
בורקס	**burekas**	turnovers filled with cheese or potatoes

VEGETABLES

ארטישוק	**artishok**	artichoke
אבוקדו	**avokado**	avocado
שעועית	**she'u'it**	beans
כרוב	**kruv**	cabbage
גזר	**gezer**	carrot
כרובית	**kruvit**	cauliflower
תירס	**tiras**	corn
מלפפון	**melafefon**	cucumber
חציל	**KHatzil**	eggplant
צ׳יפס	**chips**	French fries
תפוחי אדמה מטוגנים	**tapuKHay adama metuganim**	fried potatoes
שום	**shum**	garlic
פלפל ירוק	**pilpel yarok**	green pepper
עדשים	**adashim**	lentils
חסה	**KHasa**	lettuce
פטריות	**pitriyot**	mushrooms
זיתים	**zaytim**	olives
בצל	**batzal**	onion
אפונה	**afuna**	peas
פלפל	**pilpel**	pepper
תפוח אדמה	**tapuaKH adama**	potato
בצל ירוק	**batzal yarok**	scallions
תרד	**tered**	spinach
עגבניה	**agvanya**	tomato
קישוא	**kishu**	zucchini

ירקות	**yera<u>kot</u>**	vegetables
סלט ירקות	**sa<u>lat</u> yera<u>kot</u>**	vegetable salad
ירקות העונה	**yera<u>kot</u> ha-'o<u>na</u>**	vegetables of the season

FRUITS, NUTS, AND SEEDS

שקדים	**shke<u>dim</u>**	almonds
תפוח עץ	**tapu<u>aкн</u> etz**	apple
משמש	**mish<u>mesh</u>**	apricot
בננה	**ba<u>na</u>na**	banana
תמר	**ta<u>mar</u>**	date
תאנה	**te'e<u>na</u>**	fig
פירות	**pay<u>rot</u>**	fruit (pl.)
פרי	**pri**	fruit (sing.)
פירות העונה	**pay<u>rot</u> ha-'o<u>na</u>**	fruit of the season
ענבים	**ana<u>vim</u>**	grapes
אשכולית	**eshko<u>lit</u>**	grapefruit
לימון	**li<u>mon</u>**	lemon
מנגו	**<u>man</u>go**	mango
מלון	**me<u>lon</u>**	melon
אגוזים	**ego<u>zim</u>**	nuts, walnuts
תפוז	**ta<u>puz</u>**	orange
אפרסק	**afar<u>sek</u>**	peach
בוטנים	**bot<u>nim</u>**	peanuts
אגס	**a<u>gas</u>**	pear
אננס	**<u>a</u>nanas**	pineapple
פיסטוק חלבי	**<u>fistuk</u> кнa<u>la</u>bi**	pistachio nuts
שזיף	**she<u>zif</u>**	plum
רימון	**ri<u>mon</u>**	pomegranate

תות שדה	tut sa<u>deh</u>	strawberry
גרעינים	gar'inim	sunflower seeds
אבטיח	ava<u>ti</u>aкн	watermelon

CAKES AND DESSERTS

עוגה	<u>u</u>ga	cake
עוגת גבינה	ugat gvi<u>na</u>	cheesecake
עוגת שוקולד	ugat shoko<u>lad</u>	chocolate cake
מוס שוקולד	mus shoko<u>lad</u>	chocolate mousse
עוגיה	ugi<u>ya</u>	cookie
קרם קרמל	krem kara<u>mel</u>	crème caramel
קרם בווריה	krem ba<u>va</u>ria	custard-like dessert made from eggs and vanilla
מנה אחרונה	ma<u>na</u> aкнaro<u>na</u>	dessert
קינוח	ki<u>nu</u>aкн	dessert
סופגניה	sufgan<u>ya</u>	doughnut
סלט פירות	sa<u>lat</u> pay<u>rot</u>	fruit salad
גלידה	<u>gli</u>da	ice cream
מוס	mus	mousse
טורט	tort	rich cake
בלינצ׳ס	<u>blin</u>ches	thin pancakes filled with chocolate or sweet cheese
עוגת שמרים	u<u>gat</u> shma<u>rim</u>	yeast cake

DRINKS

משקה חריף	mash<u>keh</u> кнa<u>rif</u>	alcoholic drink
בירה	<u>bi</u>ra	beer

קפה שחור	kafeh shaKHor	black coffee
בירה בבקבוק	bira be-bakbuk	bottled beer
לבן	leben	buttermilk
בירה בפחית	bira be-paKHit	canned beer
משקה תוסס	mashkeh toses	carbonated drink
שמפניה	shampanya	champagne
שוקו קר	shoko kar	cold chocolate
שוקו חם	shoko KHam	hot chocolate
קקאו	kaka'o	cocoa
קפה	kafeh	coffee
קפה הפוך	kafeh hafuKH	coffee with milk
קפה נטול קפאין	kafeh netul kafe'in	decaffeinated coffee
בירה מהחבית	bira me-ha-KHavit	draft beer
משקה	mashkeh	drink
תה צמחים	teh tzmaKHim	herbal tea
נס קפה	nes kafeh	instant coffee
מיץ	mitz	juice
לימונדה	limonada	lemonade
חלב	KHalav	milk
מילקשייק	milkshayk	milk shake
מים מינרליים	mayim mineraliyim	mineral water
מיץ תפוזים	mitz tapuzim	orange juice
יין אדום	yayin adom	red wine
סודה	soda	soda water
משקה קל	mashkeh kal	soft drink
יין נתזים	yayn netazim	sparkling wine

קפה בוץ	**ka<u>feh</u>** botz	strong black coffee
תה	**teh**	tea
תה עם לימון	**teh im li<u>mon</u>**	tea with lemon
תה עם חלב	**teh im K<u>Ha</u>la<u>v</u>**	tea with milk
קפה תורכי/ טורקי	**ka<u>feh</u> turki**	Turkish coffee
מים	**<u>ma</u>yim**	water
יין לבן	**<u>ya</u>yin la<u>van</u>**	white wine
יין	**<u>ya</u>yin**	wine

BASIC FOODS

חמאה	**KHem<u>'a</u>**	butter
שמנת מתוקה	**sha<u>me</u>net metu<u>ka</u>**	cream
דבש	**dvash**	honey
ריבה	**ri<u>ba</u>**	jam, marmalade
מרגרינה	**marga<u>ri</u>na**	margarine
מיונז	**mayo<u>nez</u>**	mayonnaise
חרדל	**KHar<u>dal</u>**	mustard
שמן	**<u>she</u>men**	oil
שמן זית	**<u>she</u>men <u>za</u>yit**	olive oil
ריבת תפוזים	**ri<u>bat</u> tapu<u>zim</u>**	orange marmalade
אורז	**<u>o</u>rez**	rice
רוטב	**<u>ro</u>tev**	sauce, gravy
שמנת	**sha<u>me</u>net**	sour cream
חומץ	**K<u>Ho</u>metz**	vinegar
קצפת	**kat<u>zef</u>et**	whipped cream
יוגורט	**<u>yo</u>gurt**	yogurt

HERBS AND SPICES

פלפל חריף	pil<u>pel</u> к<u>нarif</u>	hot pepper or chili powder
נענע	<u>na</u>ʻana	mint
זעתר	<u>za</u>ʻatar	native thyme
פלפל	pil<u>pel</u>	pepper
מלח	<u>me</u>lakн	salt
תבלין	tav<u>lin</u>	spice, herb

TYPES OF BREAD, ETC.

לחם שחור	<u>le</u>кнem sha<u>кн</u>or	'black' (brown or whole wheat) bread
לחם	<u>le</u>кнem	bread
לחמניה	lakн<u>man</u>ya	bun, roll
חלה	<u>кна</u>la	challah—a rich, eggy Sabbath bread
מצה	mat<u>za</u>	matzo—crisp, unleavened Passover bread
פיתה	<u>pi</u>ta	pita bread
לחם חי	<u>le</u>кнem <u>кн</u>ai	wheatgerm bread
לחם לבן	<u>le</u>кнem la<u>van</u>	white bread

SNACKS

פלאפל	fa<u>la</u>fel	falafel—fried chickpea balls in pita bread with salad and hot pepper sauce
המבורגר	<u>ham</u>burger	hamburger
נקניקיה	nakni<u>ki</u>ya	hot dog
פשטידה	pash<u>ti</u><u>da</u>	pie

פיצה	**pi**tza	pizza
כריך	ka**rikh**	sandwich
סנדוויץ'	**sendvich**	sandwich

CULINARY METHODS OF PREPARATION

אפוי	**afuy**	baked
מאפה	ma**'afeh**	baked
בגריל	be-**gril**	broiled
מבושל	mevu**shal**	cooked, prepared
מטוגן	metu**gan**	fried
בתנור	ba-ta**nur**	ovenbaked
מחית	me**khit**	purée
נא	**na**	raw, rare
על האש	al ha-**'esh**	roasted, barbecued
מתובל	metu**bal**	seasoned, spicy
צלוי	tza**lui**	stewed
ממולא	memu**la**	stuffed, filled

MISCELLANEOUS

מר	**mar**	bitter
מנה	**ma**na	dish, serving, course
חריף	kha**rif**	hot, spicy
מלוח	ma**luakh**	salty
טחינה	te**khi**na	sesame seed paste
תוספות	tosa**fot**	side dishes
חמוץ	kha**mutz**	sour
מתוק	ma**tok**	sweet
עלי גפן	a**lay ge**fen	vine leaves

SHOPPING

Israel has large, sophisticated, air-conditioned department stores and shopping malls. You'll also find exotic and colorful outdoor markets, called **shuk** (שוק), which offer anything from spices to antiques. They're also the best place to buy fruits and vegetables. Bargaining is customary in the **shuk**: if you begin by offering half the required price, you will probably get a fair deal. Do not, however, try to bargain in Tel Aviv's upscale boutiques! In Jerusalem, it's advisable to seek advice about the current political situation before shopping in the eastern part of the city.

Some smaller stores and offices open at 8 or 9 AM, close for a lunch break at around 1 PM, and then reopen until 7 PM.

USEFUL WORDS AND PHRASES

audio equipment	מערכות סטריאו	*ma'araKHot ste*rio
bakery	מאפיה	*ma'afiya*
bookstore	חנות ספרים	*KHanut sfarim*
boutique	בוטיק	*butik*
butcher	אטליז	*itliz*
to buy	לקנות	*liknot*
cash register	קופה	*kupa*
department store	חנות כלבו	*KHanut kolbo*
diamond	יהלום	*yahalom*
fashion	אופנה	*ofna*
fish market	מוכר דגים	*moKHer dagim*
florist	מוכר פרחים	*moKHer praKHim*
goldsmith	צורף זהב	*tzoref zahav*
grocer	מכולת	*makolet*
grocery bag (*plastic*)	שקית נילון	*sakit nailon*

hardware store	חנות כלי בית	KHanut klay bayit
inexpensive	זול	zol
ladies' wear	בגדי נשים	bigday nashim
menswear	בגדי גברים	bigday gvarim
newsstand	מוכר עתונים	moKHer itonim
pastry shop	קונדיטוריה	konditoria
pharmacist	בית מרקחת	bayt mirkaKHat
receipt	קבלה	kabala
record and cassette store	חנות תקליטים	KHanut taklitim
rug	שטיח	shatiaKH
sale	מכירה	meKHira
sales assistant (male)	מוכר	moKHer
(female)	מוכרת	moKHeret
shoe store	חנות נעליים	KHanut na'alayim
to go shopping	לעשות קניות	la'asot kniyot
shopping cart	עגלה	agala
silversmith	צורף כסף	tzoref kesef
souvenir shop	חנות מזכרות	KHanut mazkarot
special offer	מבצע	mivtza
to spend	להוציא	lehotzi
stationery shop	חנות מכשירי כתיבה	KHanut maKHshiray ktiva
store	חנות	KHanut
supermarket	סופרמרקט	supermarket
tailor	חייט	KHayat
toy store	חנות צעצועים	KHanut tza'atzu'im
travel agent	סוכן נסיעות	soKHen nesi'ot

I'd like . . .

אני מבקש/מבקשת ...

ani mevakesh (m)/*mevakeshet* (f) . . .

Do you have . . .?

יש לך ...?

yesh leкна (to a man) . . .?

יש לך ...?

yesh laкн (to a woman) . . .?

How much is this?

כמה זה עולה?

kama zeh oleh?

That's too much

זה יותר מדי

zeh yoter midai

I'll give you . . .

אתן לך ...

eten leкна (to a man) . . .

אתן לך ...

eten laкн (to a woman) . . .

That's my best offer

זה המקסימום

zeh ha-maximum

Two for . . .
שניים ב-...
shnayim be-. . .

OK, I'll take it
בסדר, אני לוקח/לוקחת
beseder, ani lokeaкн (m)/_lokaкнat_ (f)

Can you giftwrap it, please?
עטיפת מתנה, בבקשה
atifat matana, bevakasha

Could you wrap it for me?
אפשר לעטוף את זה?
efshar la'atof et zeh?

Where is the . . . department?
איפה מחלקת ה-...?
ayfo maкнleket ha-. . .?

Do you have any more of these?
יש עוד כאלה?
yesh od ka-eleh?

I'd like to change this, please
אני מבקש/מבקשת להחליף את זה
ani mevakesh (m)/_mevakeshet_ (f) _lehaкнlif et zeh_

Have you anything larger/smaller/less expensive?
יש יותר גדול/קטן/זול?
yesh yoter gadol/katan/zol?

Does it come in other colors?
יש צבעים אחרים?
yesh tzva'im aκHerim?

May I have a receipt?
אפשר לקבל קבלה?
efshar lekabel kabala?

May I have a bag, please?
אפשר לקבל שקית, בבקשה?
efshar lekabel sakit, bevakasha?

May I try it/them on?
אפשר למדוד?
efshar limdod?

Where do I pay?
איפה אפשר לשלם?
ayfo efshar leshalem?

May I have a refund?
אפשר לקבל החזר תשלום?
efshar lekabel heκHzer tashlum?

I'm just looking
אני רק מסתכל/מסתכלת
ani rak mistakel (m)/mistakelet (f)

I'll come back later
אני אחזור יותר מאוחר
ani aκHazor yoter me'uκHar

THINGS YOU'LL SEE

מאפיה	ma'afiya	bakery
מציאה	metzi'a	bargain (noun)
חנות ספרים	кнanut sfarim	bookstore
אטליז	itliz	butcher
מחלקה	maкнlaka	department
חנות כלבו	кнanut kolbo	department store
מכירת סוף העונה	meкнirat sof ha-'ona	end of season sale
אופנה	ofna	fashion
מיצרכים	mitzraкнim	groceries
חומרי ניקוי לבית	кнomray nikui la-bayit	household cleaning materials
גלידריה	glideriya	ice cream shop
כשר	kasher	kosher
בגדי נשים	bigday nashim	ladies' clothing
מחלקת נשים	maкнleket nashim	ladies' department
קומת קרקע	komat karka	lower floor
שוק	shuk	market
בגדי גברים	bigday gvarim	menswear
לא מקבלים המחאות	lo mekablim hamкнa'ot	no checks
קונדיטוריה	konditoria	pastry shop
נא לא לגעת	na lo laga'at	please do not touch
מחיר	meкнir	price
מוזל	muzal	reduced

→

83

השכרה	hask<u>a</u>ra	rental
מכירה	me<u>кн</u>ira	sale
שירות עצמי	sher<u>u</u>t atz<u>mi</u>	self-service
חנות נעליים	<u>кн</u>an<u>u</u>t na'al<u>a</u>yim	shoe store
מבצע	miv<u>tz</u>a	special offer
מוכר סיגריות	mo<u>кн</u>er sig<u>a</u>riot	tobacco shop
צעצועים	tza'atzu'<u>im</u>	toys
סוכן נסיעות	so<u>кн</u>en nesi'<u>ot</u>	travel agent
קומה עליונה	k<u>o</u>ma ely<u>o</u>na	upper floor
ירקות	yerak<u>o</u>t	vegetables

Things You'll Hear

efshar la'<u>a</u>zor le<u>кн</u>a (*to a man*)/**la<u>кн</u>?** (*to a woman*)
May I help you?

yesh le<u>кн</u>a (*to a man*)/**la<u>кн</u>** (*to a woman*) <u>ke</u>sef yo<u>ter</u> ka<u>tan</u>?
Do you have anything smaller?

sli<u>кн</u>a, nigmar <u>la</u>nu
I'm sorry, we're out of stock

zeh kol ma she-<u>yesh</u>
This is all we have

od <u>ma</u>shehu?/zeh ha-<u>kol</u>?
Will there be anything else?

AT THE HAIRDRESSER'S

USEFUL WORDS AND PHRASES

appointment	תור	tor
bangs	פוני	poni
beard	זקן	zakan
blond	בלונדיני	blondini
blow dry	פן	fen
brush (noun)	מברשת	mivreshet
(verb)	להבריש	lehavrish
comb (noun)	מסרק	masrek
(verb)	לסרק	lesarek
conditioner	קונדישונר	kondishoner
curl	סלסול	silsul
curlers	רולים	rolim
curly	מסולסל	mesulsal
dark	כהה	keheh
dye (noun)	צבע	tzeva
(verb)	לצבוע	litzbo'a
gel	ג'יל	jel
hair	שיער	say'ar
haircut	תספורת	tisporet
hairdresser (male)	ספר	sapar
(female)	ספרית	saparit
hair dryer	מייבש שיער	mayabesh say'ar
highlights	פסים, גוונים	pasim, gvanim
long	ארוך	arokh

moustache	שפם	*safam*
part	שביל	*shvil*
perm	פרמננט	*permanent*
shampoo	שמפו	*shampo*
shave	גילוח	*giluaкн*
shaving cream	קצף גילוח	*ketzef giluaкн*
short	קצר	*katzar*
styling mousse	מוס	*mus*
wavy	גלי	*gali*

I'd like to make an appointment
אפשר בבקשה להזמין תור?
efshar bevakasha lehazmin tor?

Just a trim, please
רק ליישר, בבקשה
rak layasher, bevakasha

Not too much off
לא להוריד יותר מדי
lo lehorid yoter midai

A bit more off here, please
אפשר להוריד עוד קצת פה, בבקשה?
efshar lehorid od ktzat po, bevakasha?

I'd like a cut and blow-dry
תספורת ופן, בבקשה
tisporet ve-fen, bevakasha

I'd like a perm

פרמננט, בבקשה

permanent, bevakasha

I'd like highlights

גוונים, בבקשה

gvanim, bevakasha

THINGS YOU'LL HEAR

ayкн tirtzeh et zeh?
How would you like it? *(to a man)*

ayкн tirtzi et zeh?
How would you like it? *(to a woman)*

zeh maspik katzar?
Is that short enough?

ata rotzeh kondishoner?
Would you like any conditioner? *(to a man)*

at rotza kondishoner?
Would you like any conditioner? *(to a woman)*

THINGS YOU'LL SEE

ספר	**sapar**	barber, men's hairdresser
מספרה	**maspera**	hairdresser
סלון	**salon**	hairdressing salon
עיצוב שיער	**itzuv say'ar**	hair styling, hairdresser
גברות	**gvarot**	(for) ladies
גברים	**gvarim**	(for) men

SPORTS

Israel's most popular sports are soccer and basketball. In recent years, tennis has been gaining ground, and so have water sports, diving, sailing, windsurfing, and waterskiing. Quality hotels and sports centers offer squash and weight-lifting facilities. There are many walking trails all over the country, rock climbing is offered in the Judean desert, and Mount Hermon has a small ski resort open during the midwinter months. Bicycling is possible, although there are very few designated routes, and drivers' courtesy leaves much to be desired. Israel has only one golf course, located near Caesaria.

There is, however, no shortage of swimming pools and beaches. The swimming season in the Mediterranean is from spring to October, while Eilat caters for swimmers all year round. Topless bathing is acceptable in Eilat and on some Mediterranean beaches, although not in urban locations. Look around you to work out what the local norms are. It's advisable to swim only when a lifeguard is in attendance. A flag warning system operates on most beaches: black for absolutely no swimming, red for caution, and white (or blue and white) for all-clear.

Israel's climate is hot, and dehydration is an ever-imminent danger. During all sports activities, make sure you take plenty of drinks and wear a hat when in the sun.

USEFUL WORDS AND PHRASES

athletics	אתלטיקה	atl_etika
ball	כדור	ka_dur
beach	חוף	KHof
(for swimming)	חוף רחצה	KHof raKHa_tza
beach umbrella	שמשיה	shimshi_ya
bicycle	אופניים	of_anayim
canoe	קנו	ka_nu

88

deck chair	כסא נוח	kiseh noakн
diving (underwater)	צלילה	tzlila
diving board	קרש קפיצה	keresh kfitza
diving suit	חליפת צלילה	кнalifat tzlila
fishing	דיג	dayig
flippers	סנפירים	snapirim
goggles	משקפי שחיה	mishkafay sкнiya
golf	גולף	"golf"
golf course	אתר גולף	atar golf
gymnastics	התעמלות	hit'amlut
hockey	הוקי	hoki
jogging	ג'וגינג, ריצה	joging, ritza
lessons	שיעורים	shi'urim
mountaineering	טיפוס הרים	tipus harim
oxygen bottles	בקבוקי חמצן	bakbukay кнamtzan
pedal boat	סירת דוושות	sirat davshot
racket	רקטה, מחבט	maкнbet, raketa
riding	רכיבה	reкнiya
rowboat	סירת משוטים	sirat mashotim
to run	לרוץ	larutz
sailboard	גלשן רוח	galshan ruaкн
sailing	שיט	shayit
sand	חול	кнol
sea	ים	yam
ski	סקי	"ski"
snorkel	שנורקל	shnorkel
soccer	כדורגל	kaduregel
soccer match	משחק כדורגל	misкнak kaduregel

89

stadium	אצטדיון	*itztad<u>yon</u>*
surfboard	גלשן	*gal<u>shan</u>*
to swim	לשחות	*lis<u>KHot</u>*
swimming pool	בריכת שחיה	*bray<u>KHat</u> s<u>KHiya</u>*
tennis	טניס	*<u>tenis</u>*
tennis court	מגרש טניס	*mi<u>grash</u> <u>tenis</u>*
tennis racket	רקטה, מחבט טניס	*ma<u>KHbet</u> tenis, ra<u>keta</u>*
tent	אוהל	*<u>ohel</u>*
volleyball	כדור עף	*ka<u>dur</u> af*
walking	הליכה	*hali<u>KHa</u>*
waterskiing	סקי מים	*ski <u>mayim</u>*
water skis	מגלשי סקי מים	*migla<u>shay</u> ski <u>mayim</u>*
wave	גל	*gal*
wind	רוח	*<u>ru</u>aKH*
windsurf	גלשן רוח	*gal<u>shan</u> <u>ru</u>aKH*
yacht	יכטה	*<u>yaKHta</u>*

How do I get to the beach?

איך מגיעים לחוף?

a<u>yKH</u> magi<u>'im</u> la-<u>KHof</u>?

How deep is the water here?

מה עומק המים כאן?

ma <u>omek</u> ha-<u>ma</u>yim kan?

Is there a swimming pool here?

יש כאן בריכת שחיה?

yesh kan bray<u>KHat</u> s<u>KHiya</u>?

Is the swimming pool heated?

הבריכה מחוממת?

ha-brayкна текнимемet?

Is it safe to swim here?

בטוח לשחות כאן?

batuaкн lisкнot kan?

Can I rent a deck chair/beach umbrella?

אפשר לשכור כסא נוח/שמשיה?

efshar liskor kiseh noaкн/shimshiya?

How much does it cost per hour/day?

כמה זה עולה לשעה/ליום?

kama zeh oleh le-sha'a/le-yom?

Can I take waterskiing lessons?

אפשר לקבל שיעורים בסקי מים?

efshar lekabel shi'urim be-ski mayim?

Where can I rent . . .?

איפה אפשר לשכור ...?

ayfo efshar liskor . . .?

THINGS YOU'LL SEE

חוף	KHof	beach, coast, shore
אופניים	ofanayim	bicycles
סירות	sirot	boats
מגרש	migrash	court, sports field
ציוד	tziyud	equipment
עזרה ראשונה	ezra rishona	first aid
להשכרה	le-haskara	for rent
אסור	asur	it is forbidden
מרינה	marina	marina
אסור לצלול	asur litzlol	no diving
אסור לשחות	asur lisKHot	no swimming
מתקני ספורט	mitkanay sport	sports facilities
מרכז ספורט	merkaz sport	sports center
אצטדיון	itztadyon	stadium
חוף רחצה (מורשה)	KHof rakHatza (mursheh)	(authorized) swimming beach
השחיה אסורה	ha-sKHiya asura	swimming prohibited
מגרש טניס	migrash tenis	tennis court
כרטיסים	kartisim	tickets
ספורט מים	sport mayim	water sports

POST OFFICES AND BANKS

Post offices can be recognized by the word דואר (doar) meaning "post" and by the symbol of a deer. Mailboxes are usually red. In some large cities, you'll also see yellow mailboxes which are intended for local mail only. Post offices in Israel are open every morning between approximately 8:30 AM and 12 noon, and most are open in the afternoons from 3:30 to 6 PM except on Fridays. Many post offices are closed for one additional afternoon a week. Israelis use the post office not only to buy stamps and send packages, but to pay bills and purchase phonecards (see Telephones, p. 98). The main post offices in large cities have a poste restante and a telephone service for calling abroad, since most pay phones cannot be used for overseas calls.

Banks in Israel are open every morning and in the afternoon from 4 to 5:30 PM The Israeli unit of currency is the **shekel** (**shekel** שקל), which is divided into 100 **agorot** (singular **agora** אגורה). If you want to change shekels back into foreign currency, it is advisable to plan your purchase in advance.

agora/agorot	אגורה/אגורות	agora/agorot
airmail	דואר אוויר	doar avir
bank	בנק	"bank"
bills (currency)	שטר כסף	shtar kesef
to change	להחליף, להמיר	lehaкнlif, lehamir
check	שק, ציק	shek, chek
collection	איסוף דואר	isuf doar
counter	דלפק	dalpak,
customs form	טופס מכס	tofes meкнes
delivery	חלוקה	кнaluka
deposit	הפקדה	hafkada

93

dollar	דולר	_dolar_
exchange rate	שער חליפין	sha'ar кнali_fin_
form	טופס	_tofes_
international money order	המחאת כסף בינלאומית	hamкнa_'at_ ke_sef_ baynle'u_mit_
letter	מכתב	miкн_tav_
mail	דואר	_doar_
mailbox	תיבת מכתבים	tay_yat_ miкнta_vim_
mail carrier	דוור	da_var_
money	כסף	ke_sef_
money order	המחאת כסף	hamкнa_'at_ ke_sef_
overseas	חו״ל, לחו״ל	кнul, le-кнul
package	חבילה	кнavi_la_
P.O. box	תיבת דואר	tay_yat_ _doar_
post	דואר	_doar_
postage rates	דמי דואר, מחיר משלוח	dmay _doar_, meкнir mish_loa_кн
postal order	המחאת דואר	hamкнa_'at_ _doar_
postcard	גלויה	glu_ya_
poste restante	דואר שמור	_doar_ sha_mur_
post office	סניף דואר	snif _doar_
registered letter	מכתב רשום	miкн_tav_ ra_shum_
shekel	שקל	_shekel_
stamp	בול	bul
surface mail	דואר ים	_doar_ yam
telegram	מברק	miv_rak_
traveler's check	טרבלרס ציקים	_travelers_ chekim
zip code	מיקוד	mi_kud_

How much is a letter/postcard to . . .?

כמה עולה לשלוח מכתח/גלויה ל...?

kama oleh lishloaкн miкнtav/gluya le-. . .?

I would like a stamp for a postcard to the United States

אפשר לקבל בול לגלויה לארצות הברית?

efshar lekabel bul le-gluya le-arzot habrit?

I want to register this letter

אבקש לשלוח מכתב זה בדואר רשום

avakesh lishloaкн miкнtav zeh be-doar rashum

I want to send this package to . . .

אבקש לשלוח חבילה זאת ל...

avakesh lishloaкн кнavila zot le-. . .

Where can I mail this?

איפה אפשר לשלוח את זה?

ayfo efshar lishloaкн et zeh?

Is there any mail for me?

יש דואר בשבילי?

yesh doar bishvili?

I'd like to send a telegram

אבקש לשלוח מברק

avakesh lishloaкн mivrak

This is to go airmail

דואר אוויר בבקשה

doar avir bevakasha

I'd like to change this into . . .

אבקש להחליף את זה ל...

avakesh lehakHlif et zeh le-. . .

Can I cash these traveler's checks?

אפשר להמיר את טרבלרס צקים האלה?

efshar lehamir et ha'travelers chekim ha-nos'im ha-eleh?

What is the exchange rate for the US dollar?

מה שער החליפין לדולר?

ma sha'ar ha-kHalifin la-dolar?

THINGS YOU'LL SEE

מען, כתובת	*ma'an, ketovet*	address
נמען	*nim'an*	addressee
דואר אוויר	*doar avir*	airmail
בנק	"bank"	bank
עמלה	*amla*	charge
איסוף דואר	*isuf doar*	collection times
בול בתוך הארץ	*bul betokH ha-aretz*	domestic postage
החלפת מטבע זר	*hakHlafat matbe'a zar*	exchange office
דואר אקספרס, דואר מהיר	*doar ekspres, doar mahir*	express
הרקה אחרונה	*haraka akHrona*	last collection
מכתב	*mikHtav*	letter

→

תיבת דואר, תיבת מכתבים	tayvat doar, tayvat miкнtavim	mailbox
המחאות כסף	hamкнa'ot kesef	money orders
שעות פתיחה	sha'ot petiкнa	opening hours
דלפק חבילות	dalpak кнavilot	packages counter
מחיר משלוח, דמי דואר	meкнir mishloaкн, dmay doar	postage
בול לחו״ל, מחיר משלוח לחו״ל	bul le-кнul, meкнir mishloaкн le-кнul	postage abroad
דואר שמור	doar shamur	poste restante
דואר	doar	post office
דואר רשום	doar rashum	registered mail
שולח	sholeaкн	sender
בולים	bul/bulim	stamp/s
מברקים	mivrakim	telegrams
מיקוד	mikud	zip code

TELEPHONES

Israel's government-controlled telephone network, **Bezek**
(בזק), which gradually improved a dated and over-congested
system, has now been partially privatized. The system has now
gone fully digital and a high percentage of people use cell
phones. Pay phones will take coins and phonecards and some
also allow payment by credit card. Direct dialing is available to
most countries. Some pay phones may not yet be equipped for
dialling abroad, unless you ask the operator for a collect call.
International calls can be made from most pay phones, and
from private telephones or central post offices.

USEFUL WORDS AND PHRASES

call	שיחת טלפון	si<small>KH</small>at telefon
to call	לטלפן	letalpen
code	קידומת	kidomet
collect call	גוביינא, קולקט	govaina, kolekt
crossed line	תקלה בקוים	takala ba-kavim
to dial	לחייג	leKHayeg
dial tone	צליל חיוג	tzlil KHiyug
directory assistance	מודיעין	modi'in
emergency	חירום	mikray KHerum
extension	שלוחה	shluKHa
international call	שיחה בינלאומית	siKHa baynle'umit
local call	שיחה מקומית	siKHa mekomit
long-distance call	שיחה בין עירונית	siKHa bayn ironit
number	מספר	mispar
operator	מרכזיה	merkaziya
pay phone	טלפון ציבורי	telefon tziburi
phone book	מדריך טלפון	madriKH telefon

phone booth	תא טלפון	ta telefon
phonecard	טלקרד	telecard
receiver	שפופרת	shfoferet
telephone	טלפון	telefon
wrong number	טעות במספר	ta'ut ba-mispar

Where is the nearest phone booth?
איפה תא הטלפון הקרוב?
ayfo ta ha-telefon ha-karov?

Is there a phone book?
יש מדריך טלפון?
yesh madriKH telefon?

I would like the directory for . . .
אפשר לקבל את המדריך לאיזור ...?
efshar lekabel et ha-madriKH le-ayzor . . .?

Can I call abroad from here?
אפשר לטלפן מכאן לחו"ל?
efshar letalpen mikan le-KHul?

How much is a call to . . .?
כמה עולה שיחה ל...?
kama ola siKHa le-. . .?

I would like to make a collect call
אבקש לטלפן קולקט
avakesh letalpen kolekt

I would like a number in . . .
...אבקש למצוא מספר ב
avakesh limtzo mispar be-. . .

Hello, this is . . . speaking
... שלום, מדבר/מדברת
shalom, medaber (m)/*medaberet* (f) . . .

Is that . . .?
?...זה/זו
zeh (to a man)/*zo* (to a woman) . . .?

Speaking
מדבר/מדברת
medaber (m)/*medaberet* (f)

May I speak to . . .?
?...אפשר לדבר עם
efshar ledaber im . . .?

Extension . . ., please
שלוחה ..., בבקשה
shluKHa . . ., bevakasha

Please tell him/her . . . called

בבקשה למסור לו/לה ש... טלפן

bevakasha limsor lo/la she-. . . tilpen (if a man called)

בבקשה למסור לו/לה ש... טלפנה

bevakasha limsor lo/la she-. . . tilpena (if a woman called)

Ask him to call me back, please

אפשר לבקש שיחזיר צלצול, בבקשה?

efshar levakesh she-yaKHzir tziltzul, bevakasha?

My number is . . .

... המספר שלי הוא

hamispar sheli hu . . .

Do you know where he is?

אתה יודע איפה הוא?

ata yode'a ayfo hu? (to a man)

את יודעת איפה הוא?

at yoda'at ayfo hu? (to a woman)

When will he be back?

מתי הוא יחזור?

matai hu yaKHzor?

Could you leave a message?

אפשר להשאיר הודעה?

efshar lehash'ir hoda'a?

I'll call back later

אתקשר שוב אחר כך

etka<u>sher</u> shuv a<u>KHar</u> ka<u>KH</u>

Sorry, wrong number

סליחה, טעות במספר

sli<u>KHa</u>, ta'<u>ut</u> bami<u>spar</u>

THINGS YOU'LL SEE

בזק	<u>be</u>zek	Bezek
שירות תיקונים	shay<u>rut</u> tiku<u>nim</u>	complaints department
חיוג ישיר	<u>KH</u>i<u>yug</u> ya<u>shir</u>	direct dialing
מודיעין	modi'<u>in</u>	directory assistance
חירום	<u>KHe</u>rum	emergency
בינלאומי	baynle'<u>umi</u>	international
מרכזייה	merka<u>ziya</u>	operator
מקולקל	mekul<u>kal</u>	out of order
טלפון	<u>te</u>lefon	telephone

THINGS YOU'LL HEAR

et mi ata rotzeh? *(to a man)*
et mi at rotza? *(to a woman)*
Whom would you like to speak to?

ta'ut ba-mispar
You've got the wrong number

mi medaber *(to a man)*/**medaberet** *(to a woman)*?
Who's speaking?

ma ha-mispar shelKHa *(to a man)*/**shelaKH** *(to a woman)*?
What is your number?

hu lo nimtza/hi lo nimtzet
He's not in/she's not in

hu yaKHzor be-. . .
He'll be back at . . . o'clock

hi taKHzor be-. . .
She'll be back at . . . o'clock

titkasher *(to a man)*/**titkashri** *(to a woman)* **shuv maKHar**
Please call again tomorrow

ani agid lo/la she-tilpanta *(to a man)*
I'll tell him/her you called

ani agid lo/la she-tilpant *(to a woman)*
I'll tell him/her you called

HEALTH

Israel has a very high standard of health care. While the doctor's bedside manner may at times seem less than courteous, you can count on first-rate care in hospitals and clinics. All travelers must be insured to cover illness, accidents, and any subsequent hospitalization. Most doctors practice in clinics called **kupat kholim** (קופת חולים), where there are general practitioners as well as specialists. The public first-aid and ambulance service, **magen david adom** (מגן דוד אדום), should be contacted for emergencies.

All fruits and vegetables should be washed thoroughly to avoid any stomach problems. If traveling in the summer, the sun can be extremely dangerous, particularly for fair-skinned Europeans and North Americans. It is advisable to wear a hat when in the sun and drink plenty of fluids to avoid sunstroke and dehydration.

USEFUL WORDS AND PHRASES

accident	תאונה	te'una
ambulance	אמבולנס	ambulans
anemic	אנמי	anemi
appendicitis	דלקת תוספתן, אפנדיציט	daleket toseftan, apenditzit
asthma	אסתמה	astma
backache	כאב גב	ke'ev gav
bandage	תחבושת	takhboshet
bandage (adhesive)	פלסתר, אגד מדבק	plaster, eged medabek
bite (by dog)	נשיכה	neshikha
(by insect)	עקיצה	akitza
bladder	שלפוחית	shalpukhit
blood	דם	dam

blood donor	תורם דם	torem dam
burn	כוויה	keviya
cancer	סרטן	sartan
chest	חזה	KHazeh
chicken pox	אבעבועות רוח	aba'abu'ot ruaKH
cholera	חולירע	KHolira
clinic	מרפאה	mirpa'ah
cold	הצטננות	hitztanenut
concussion	זעזוע מוח	za'azu'a moaKH
constipation	עצירות	atzirut
corn	יבלת	yabelet
cough	שיעול	shi'ul
cut	חתך	KHataKH
dentist (male)	רופא שיניים	rofeh shinayim
(female)	רופאת שיניים	rof'at shinayim
diabetes	סכרת	sakeret
diarrhea	שלשול	shilshul
dizziness	סחרחורת	sKHarKHoret
doctor (male)	רופא	rofeh
(female)	רופאה	rof'ah
(form of address)	דוקטור	doktor
earache	כאב אוזניים	ke'ev oznayim
fever	חום	KHom
filling	סתימה	stima
first aid	עזרה ראשונה	ezra rishona
flu	שפעת	shapa'at
fracture	שבר	shever
gastroenteritis	דלקת קיבה	daleket kayva

HEALTH

German measles	אדמת	ademet
hay fever	קדחת השחת, אלרגיה	kadaKHat ha-shaKHat, elergia
headache	כאב ראש	ke'ev rosh
heart	לב	lev
heart attack	התקף לב	hetkef lev
hemorrhage	דימום	dimum
hospital	בית חולים	bayt KHolim
ill	חולה	KHoleh (m), KHolah (f)
indigestion	קלקול קיבה	kilkul kayva
kidney	כליה	klaya
lump	גוש	gush
malaria	קדחת	kadaKHat
measles	חצבת	KHatzevet
migraine	מיגרנה, כאב ראש	migrena, ke'ev rosh
motion sickness	מחלת ים	maKHalat yam
mumps	חזרת	KHazeret
nausea	בחילה	beKHila
nurse (male)	אח	aKH
(female)	אחות	aKHot
operation	ניתוח	nituaKH
pain	כאב	ke'ev
penicillin	פניצילין	penitzilin
pharmacist	בית מרקחת	bayt mirkaKHat
plaster of Paris	גבס	geves
pneumonia	דלקת ריאות	daleket rayot
pregnant	בהריון	be-herayon
prescription	מרשם	mirsham

rheumatism	שיגרון	shiga_ron_
scald	כוויה	keviy_a_
scratch	סריטה	sri_ta_
sore throat	כאב גרון	ke'ev garo_n_
splinter	קוץ	kotz
sting	עקיצה	akit_za_
stomach	בטן	_beten_
temperature	חום	KHom
tonsils	שקדים	shke_dim_
toothache	כאב שיניים	ke'ev shina_yim_
ulcer	כיב	kiv
vaccination	חיסון	KHisu_n_
to vomit	להקיא	lehak_i_
whooping cough	שעלת	sha'elet
yellow fever	קדחת צהובה	kada_KH_at tzehu_ba_

I have a pain in . . .
יש לי כאבים ב...
yesh li ke'evi_m_ ba-. . .

I don't feel well
אני מרגיש/מרגישה לא טוב
_ani margi_sh_ (m)/margi_sha_ (f) lo tov

I feel faint
אני מרגיש חלש
_ani margish KHala_sh_ (m)

אני מרגישה חלשה
_ani margi_sha_ KHala_sha_ (f)

I feel sick
יש לי בחילות
yesh li beKHilot

I feel dizzy
יש לי סחרחורת
yesh li sKHarKHoret

I need to go to the clinic
אני צריך ללכת למרפאה
ani tzariKH laleKHet le-mirpa'a (m)

אני צריכה ללכת למרפאה
ani tzriKHa laleKHet le-mirpa'a (f)

It hurts here
כואב לי פה
ko'ev li po

It's a sharp/dull pain
זה כאב חד/עמום
zeh ke'ev KHad/amum

It hurts all the time
כואב כל הזמן
ko'ev kol ha-zman

It only hurts now and then
כואב לפעמים
ko'ev lifa'amim

It hurts when you touch it

כואב כשנוגעים

ko*'ev* ke-she-nog*'im*

It hurts more at night

כואב יותר בלילה

ko*'ev* yoter ba-*laila*

It stings

זה צורב

zeh tzo*rev*

It aches

כואב לי

ko*'ev* li

I have a temperature

יש לי חום

yesh li кном

I need a prescription for . . .

אני צריך/צריכה מרשם ל...

ani tza*ri*кн (m)/tzri*kн*a (f) mir*sham* le-. . .

I normally take . . .

אני בדרך כלל לוקח ...

ani be-*de*reкн klal lo*kea*кн . . . (m)

אני בדרך כלל לוקחת ...

ani be-*de*reкн klal lo*ka*кнat . . . (f)

I'm allergic to . . .
יש לי אלרגיה ל...
yesh li <u>alergia</u> le-. . .

Have you got anything for . . .?
יש משהו ל...?
yesh <u>ma</u>-she-hu le-. . .?

Do I need a prescription for . . .?
צריך מרשם ל...?
tza<u>ri</u>KH mir<u>sham</u> le-. . .?

I have lost a filling
אבדה לי סתימה
av<u>da</u> li sti<u>ma</u>

THINGS YOU'LL SEE

אמבולנס	<u>ambulans</u>	ambulance
מרפאה	mirpa‘ah	clinic
רופא שיניים	rofeh shin<u>ay</u>im	dentist (male)
רופאת שיניים	rof‘<u>at</u> shin<u>ay</u>im	dentist (female)
רופא	ro<u>feh</u>	doctor (male)
רופאה	rof‘<u>ah</u>	doctor (female)
דוקטור (ד״ר)	<u>dok</u>tor	doctor (Dr.) (title)
מרפאה	mirpa‘ah	doctor's office
תחנת עזרה ראשונה	таKHanat <u>ezra</u> rish<u>ona</u>	first aid post

→

קופת חולים	kupat кнolim	general health-care clinic
בית חולים	bayt кнolim	hospital
תרופה	tru<u>fa</u>	medicine
בקיבה ריקה	be-kay<u>va</u> ray<u>ka</u>	on an empty stomach
אופטיקאי	opti<u>kai</u>	optician
רוקח	ro<u>kea</u>кн	pharmacist
מגן דוד אדום	ma<u>gen</u> da<u>vid</u> <u>adom</u>	public first aid and ambulance service

THINGS YOU'LL HEAR

kaкн *(to a man)*/**ke<u>кн</u>i** *(to a woman)* . . . **kadu<u>rim</u> kol <u>pa</u>'am**
Take . . . pills at a time

im <u>ma</u>yim
With water

<u>pa</u>'am a<u>кн</u>at be-<u>yom</u>
Once a day

pa'a<u>ma</u>yim be-<u>yom</u>
Twice a day

sha<u>losh</u> pe'a<u>mim</u> be-<u>yom</u>
Three times a day

ma a<u>ta</u> lo<u>kea</u>кн be-<u>de</u>reкн klal? *(to a man)*
ma at lo<u>ka</u>кнat be-<u>de</u>reкн klal? *(to a woman)*
What do you normally take?

le-zeh tza<u>riкн</u> mir<u>sham</u>
For that you need a prescription

111

CONVERSION TABLES

DISTANCES

Distances are marked in kilometers. To convert kilometers to miles, divide the km by 8 and multiply by 5 (one km being five-eighths of a mile). Convert miles to km by dividing the miles by 5 and multiplying by 8. A mile is 1609 m (1.609 km).

km	miles or km	miles
1.61	1	0.62
3.22	2	1.24
4.83	3	1.86
6.44	4	2.48
8.05	5	3.11
9.66	6	3.73
11.27	7	4.35
12.88	8	4.97
14.49	9	5.59
16.10	10	6.21

Other units of length:

1 centimeter = 0.39 in	1 inch = 25.4 millimeters
1 meter = 39.37 in	1 foot = 0.30 meter (30 cm)
10 meter = 32.81 ft	1 yard = 0.91 meter

WEIGHTS

The unit you will come into most contact with is the kilogram (kilo), equivalent to 2 lb 3oz. To convert kg to lbs, multiply by 2 and add one-tenth of the result (thus, 6 kg x 2 = 12 + 1.2, or 13.2 lbs). One ounce is about 28 grams, and 1 lb is 454 g.

grams	ounces	ounces	grams
50	1.76	1	28.3
100	3.53	2	56.7
250	8.81	4	113.4
500	17.63	8	226.8

		lbs	
	kg	or kg	lbs
	0.45	1	2.20
	0.91	2	4.41
	1.36	3	6.61
	1.81	4	8.82
	2.27	5	11.02
	2.72	6	13.23
	3.17	7	15.43
	3.63	8	17.64
	4.08	9	19.84
	4.53	10	22.04

TEMPERATURE

To convert centigrade or Celsius degrees into Fahrenheit, the accurate method is to multiply the C° figure by 1.8 and add 32. Similarly, to convert F° to C°, subtract 32 from the F° figure and divide by 1.8. This will give you a truly accurate conversion, but takes a little time in mental arithmetic! See the table below.

C°	F°	C°	F°	
-10	14	25	77	
0	32	30	86	
5	41	36.9	98.6	body temperature
10	50	40	104	
20	68	100	212	boiling point

LIQUIDS

One "imperial" gallon is roughly 4.5 liters, but American
drivers must remember that the US gallon is only 3.8 liters
(1 liter = 1.06 US quart). In the following table, US gallons
are used:

liters	gals *or* l	gals
3.77	1	0.27
7.54	2	0.53
11.31	3	0.80
15.08	4	1.06
18.85	5	1.33
22.62	6	1.59
26.39	7	1.86
30.16	8	2.12
33.93	9	2.37
37.70	10	2.65
75.40	20	5.31
113.10	30	7.96
150.80	40	10.61
188.50	50	13.26

TIRE PRESSURES

lb/sq in	15	18	20	22	24
kg/sq cm	1.1	1.3	1.4	1.5	1.7

lb/sq in	26	28	30	33	35
kg/sq cm	1.8	2.0	2.1	2.3	2.5

MINI-DICTIONARY

about: about 16 be-ереkн shesh
    esreh
accelerator davshat ha-delek
accident te'una
accommodations megurim
ache ke'ev
adaptor (electrical) ma'avir кнashmali
address ktovet
adhesive niyar devek
after акнаray
aftershave after shayv
again od pa'am
against (opposing) neged
air conditioning mizug avir
aircraft matos
air freshener metaher avir
airline кнеvrat te'ufa
airport sdeh te'ufa
alcohol mashkeh кнarif
all kol
    all the streets kol ha-reкнovot
    that's all, thanks zeh ha-kol, toda
almost kim'at
alone levad
already kvar
always tamid
am: I am ani
ambulance ambulans
America amerika
American (man, adj.) amerika'i
    (woman) amerika'it
Amman rabat amon
ancient atik
and veh-. . .
ankle karsol
anorak me'il geshem kal
another (different) акнеr
    (additional) od

antiques store кнanut atikot
antiquities atikot
antiseptic (solution) кнomer кнitui
apartment dira
aperitif aperitif
appetite te'avon
apple tapuakн etz
application form tofes bakasha
appointment pgisha
    (medical) tor
apricot mishmesh
Arab (man, adj.) aravi
    (woman) araviya
Arabic aravit
archaeological excavation кнafira
    аркне'ologit
archaeological site atar аркне'ologi
are: you are ata (to a man)/
    at (to a woman)
    we are anaкнnu
    they are hem (m)/hen (f)
arm zro'a
army tzava
art omanut
art gallery galeria le-omanut
artist oman
as: as soon as possible ba-mehirut
    ha-efsharit
ashtray ma'afera
asleep yashen
aspirin aspirin
at: at the post office ba-do'ar
    at night ba-laila
attractive yafeh
aunt doda
Australia ostralia
Australian (man, adj.) ostrali
    (woman) ostralit

115

Austria o<u>s</u>tria
away: is it far away? zeh ra<u>кн</u>ok?
  go away! le<u>кн</u> *(to a man)*/
  le<u>кн</u>i *(to a woman)* mi<u>po</u>!
awful n<u>o</u>ra
ax gar<u>zen</u>
axle tzir

baby ti<u>no</u>k *(m)*/tino<u>ke</u>t *(f)*
baby carriage e<u>g</u>lat ti<u>no</u>k
back *(not front)* a<u>кн</u>or
  (body) gav
  (adj.) a<u>кн</u>ori
backgammon shesh besh
backpack tar<u>mil</u> gav
bad ra
baggage mit<u>'an</u>
baggage rack ma<u>daf</u> mit<u>'an</u>
baggage room shmi<u>rat</u>
  <u>кн</u>afa<u>tzim</u>
bake le'e<u>fot</u>
baker o<u>fe</u>h
balcony mir<u>pe</u>set
ball *(football, etc.)* ka<u>du</u>r
ballpoint pen et kadu<u>ri</u>
banana ba<u>na</u>na
band *(pop, rock)* laha<u>ka</u>
  (brass) tiz<u>mo</u>ret
bandage ta<u>кн</u><u>bo</u>shet
  (adhesive) <u>pla</u>ster
bank bank
bar bar
  bar of chocolate tav<u>lat</u> shoko<u>lad</u>
barbecue <u>bar</u>bekiu
bargain *(noun)* metzi<u>'a</u>
  (verb) la'a<u>mod</u> al ha-<u>me</u>kaкн
basement mar<u>tef</u>
basket sal
bath am<u>ba</u>tia
  to have a bath la'a<u>sot</u> am<u>ba</u>tia
bathing cap <u>ko</u>va ra<u>кн</u>a<u>tza</u>
bathing suit <u>be</u>ged yam

bathroom <u>кн</u>a<u>dar</u> am<u>ba</u>tia
battery sole<u>la</u>, ba<u>te</u>ria
bazaar ba<u>zar</u>, shuk
beach <u>кн</u>of
  (for swimming) <u>кн</u>of ra<u>кн</u>a<u>tza</u>
beans sheu'<u>it</u>
beard za<u>kan</u>
because ki, big<u>lal</u>
bed mi<u>ta</u>
bed linen k<u>lay</u> mi<u>ta</u>
bedroom <u>кн</u>a<u>dar</u> shay<u>na</u>
beef ba<u>kar</u>
beer <u>bi</u>ra
before lif<u>nay</u>, <u>ko</u>dem
  before the summer lif<u>nay</u> ha-<u>ka</u>yitz
  I was here before ha<u>yi</u>ti kan
  <u>ko</u>dem
beginner mat<u>кн</u>il *(m)*/mat<u>кн</u>i<u>la</u> *(f)*
behind . . . me'a<u>кн</u>a<u>ray</u> . . .
  she was left behind hi nish'a<u>ra</u>
  me'a<u>кн</u>or
beige <u>be</u>zн
Beirut bay<u>rut</u>
bell pa'a<u>mon</u>
below le<u>ma</u>ta, mi<u>ta</u><u>кн</u>at
  he is waiting below hu me<u>кн</u>a<u>ke</u>
  le<u>ma</u>ta
  (it is) below zero mi<u>ta</u><u>кн</u>at la-<u>e</u>fes
belt <u>кн</u>a<u>go</u>ra
beside al yad, le<u>yad</u>
best ha-<u>tov</u> bayo<u>ter</u>
Bethlehem bayt <u>le</u><u>кн</u>em
better tov yo<u>ter</u>
between bayn
bicycle ofa<u>na</u>yim
big ga<u>dol</u>
bikini bi<u>ki</u>ni
bill *(restaurant, etc.)* <u>кн</u>esh<u>bon</u>
  (currency) shtar
bird tzi<u>por</u>
birthday yom hu<u>le</u>det
  happy birthday! yom hu<u>le</u>det
  same<u>a</u><u>кн</u>!

birthday present mat<u>nat</u> yom
  hu<u>le</u>det
bite (*noun: by dog*) neshi<u>кна</u>
  (*by insect*) aki<u>tza</u>
  (*verb*) linsho<u>кн</u>
bitter mar
black sha<u>кнor</u>
blackberry u<u>кнmania</u>
blanket smi<u>кна</u>
bleach (*noun: for cleaning*)
  hav<u>hara</u> malbin
  (*verb: hair*) lehav<u>hir</u>
blind (*cannot see*) iver
blister ya<u>belet</u>
blood dam
blouse <u>кнultza</u>
blue ka<u>кнol</u>
boat (*large*) sfina
  (*small*) sira
body guf
boil (*verb*) lehartia<u>кн</u>
bolt (*noun: on door*) man<u>'ul</u>
  (*verb*) lin<u>'ol</u>
bone <u>etzem</u>
book (*noun*) <u>sefer</u>
  (*verb*) lehaz<u>min</u>
bookstore <u>кнanut</u> sfa<u>rim</u>
boot ma<u>gaf</u>
  rubber boots maga<u>fay</u> <u>gumi</u>
border gvul
boring mesha'a<u>mem</u>
born: I was born in . . .
  no<u>la</u>deti be-. . .
both: both of them shnay<u>hem</u>
  both of us shnay<u>nu</u>
  both . . . and . . .
  gam . . . ve-gam . . .
bottle bak<u>buk</u>
bottle opener pot<u>кнan</u> bakbu<u>kim</u>
bottom ta<u>кнtit</u>
  (*sea*) karka'<u>it</u>
bowl ke'a<u>ra</u>
box kuf<u>sa</u>

boy (*young*) <u>yeled</u>
  (*older*) na'ar
boyfriend <u>кнaver</u>
bra <u>кнaziya</u>
bracelet tza<u>mid</u>
brake (*noun*) breks
  (*verb*) liv<u>lom</u>
brandy <u>brendi</u>, <u>koniak</u>
bread le<u>кнem</u>
breakdown (*car*) pan<u>cher</u>
  (*nervous*) hitmote<u>tut</u> atza<u>bim</u>
breakfast aru<u>кнat</u> boker
breathe lin<u>shom</u>
  I can't breathe ka<u>sheh</u> li
  lin<u>shom</u>
bridge <u>gesher</u>
briefcase mizva<u>da</u>
British <u>briti</u> (*m*)/<u>britit</u> (*f*)
brochure (*tourist*) <u>кнoveret</u> may<u>da</u>
broil gril
broken sha<u>vur</u>
  broken leg <u>regel</u> shvu<u>ra</u>
brooch si<u>kat</u> noy
brother a<u>кн</u>
brown <u>кнum</u>
bruise (*noun*) <u>кнabura</u>
brush (*noun*) miv<u>reshet</u>
  (*verb*) lehav<u>rish</u>
bucket dli
building bin<u>yan</u>
bumper pa<u>gosh</u>
burglar po<u>retz</u>
burn (*noun*) keviya
  (*verb*) lis<u>rof</u>
bus oto<u>bus</u>
business <u>esek</u>
  it's none of your business
  zeh lo iske<u>кна</u>
bus station та<u>кнanat</u> oto<u>bus</u>
busy (*person*) a<u>suk</u> (*m*)/
  a<u>suka</u> (*f*)
  (*crowded*) so'<u>en</u>
but a<u>val</u>

butcher kat<u>zav</u>
butter KHem<u>'a</u>
button kaf<u>tor</u>
buy lik<u>not</u>
by: by the window leyad ha-KHa<u>lon</u>
  by Friday ad yom shi<u>shi</u>
  by myself leva<u>di</u>

cabbage kruv
cabinet a<u>ron</u>
café bayt ka<u>feh</u>
Cairo ka<u>hir</u>
cake u<u>ga</u>
calculator maKH<u>shev</u> kis
call: what's it called? ayKH kor<u>'im</u>
  la-zeh?
camel ga<u>mal</u>
camera matzle<u>ma</u>
camper *(vehicle)* kara<u>van</u>
campsite <u>kam</u>ping
camshaft mim<u>seret</u>
can *(tin)* paKHit
can: can I have . . .?
  ef<u>shar</u> leka<u>bel</u> . . .?
Canada <u>ka</u>nada
Canadian *(man, adj.)* ka<u>na</u>di
  (woman) ka<u>na</u>dit
cancer sar<u>tan</u>
candle ner
candy mam<u>tak</u>
canoe ka<u>nu</u>, ka<u>yak</u>
can opener potKHan kufsa<u>'ot</u>
cap *(bottle)* mik<u>seh</u>
  (hat) <u>ko</u>va
car meKHo<u>nit</u>
carbonated to<u>ses</u>
carburetor karbu<u>rator</u>
card kar<u>tis</u>
cardigan <u>sve</u>der im kaf<u>torim</u>
careful za<u>hir</u>
  be careful! zehi<u>rut</u>!
carpet shatiaKH

carrot ge<u>zer</u>
cash mezuma<u>nim</u>
  (coins) matbe<u>'ot</u>
  to pay cash lesha<u>lem</u> bimzu<u>man</u>
cassette ka<u>letet</u>
cassette player radio tayp
castle ti<u>ra</u>
cat KHa<u>tul</u>
cathedral kated<u>rala</u>
Catholic ka<u>to</u>li *(m)*/ka<u>to</u>lit *(f)*
cauliflower kru<u>vit</u>
cave me'a<u>ra</u>
cemetery bayt kva<u>rot</u>
center mer<u>kaz</u>
certificate te'u<u>da</u>
chair ki<u>seh</u>
chambermaid KHadra<u>nit</u>
chamber music <u>mu</u>sika <u>ka</u>merit
change *(noun: money returned)* o<u>def</u>
  (small) <u>ke</u>sef ka<u>tan</u>
  (verb: clothes) le-haKH<u>lif</u> bega<u>dim</u>
check chek
checkbook pin<u>kas</u> <u>che</u>kim
cheers! *(toast)* leKHa<u>yim</u>!
cheese gvi<u>na</u>
cherry duvde<u>van</u>
chess shaKH<u>mat</u>
chest KHa<u>zeh</u>
chewing gum <u>mas</u>tik
chicken tarne<u>golet</u>
  (meat) off
child <u>ye</u>led *(m)*/<u>yal</u>da *(f)*
children yela<u>dim</u> *(m)*/yela<u>dot</u> *(f)*
china KHar<u>sina</u>
China sin
Chinese *(man, adj.)* <u>si</u>ni
  (woman) <u>si</u>nit
chocolate shoko<u>lad</u>
  box of chocolates bonbony<u>era</u>
chop *(food)* <u>tze</u>la
  (to cut) laKH<u>tokh</u>
Christ <u>ye</u>shu
Christian not<u>zri</u> *(m)*/notz<u>riya</u> *(f)*

Christianity natzrut
Christmas кнag ha-molad
church knesiya
cigar sigar
cigarette sigaria
city ir
city center merkaz ha-ir
classical music musika klasit
clean naki
clear (obvious) barur
  (water) tzalul
  is that clear? zeh barur?
clever кнакнam
clock sha'on
  (alarm) sha'on me'orer
close (near) karov
  (stuffy) makнnik
  (verb) lisgor
  the shop is closed
    ha-кнanut sgura
clothes bgadim
club mo'adon
  (cards) tiltan
clutch klach
coach (bus) otobus
  (of train) karon
coach station такнana merkazit
coast кнof
coastal: the coastal plateau
  mishor ha-кнof
coat me'il
coathanger kolav
cockroach juk
coffee kafeh
coin matbe'a
cold (illness) hitztanenut
  (adj.) metzunan
collar tzavaron
collection (stamps, etc.) osef
color tzeva
color film seret tziv'oni
comb (noun) masrek
  (verb) lesarek

come lavo
  I come from . . .
    ani ba me-. . . (m)/ani ba'a me-. . . (f)
  we came last week banu ba-shavu'a
    she-'avar
  come here! bo hena! (to a man)/
    bo'i hena! (to a woman)
compact disc taklitor
compartment ta
complicated mesubaкн
computer makнshev
computer disk disk makнshev
concert kontzert
conditioner (hair) kondishoner
condom kondom
conductor (bus) mevaker kartisim
  (orchestra) menatze'aкн
congratulations! mazal tov!
constipation atzirut
consulate konsulia
contact lenses adashot maga
contraceptive emtza'i meni'a
cook (noun) tabaкн (m)/ tabaкнit (f)
  (verb) levashel
cookie ugiya
cooking utensils klay bishul
cool karir
cork pkak
corkscrew кнoletz pkakim
corner pina
corridor misderon
cosmetics kosmetika
cost (verb) la'alot
  what does it cost? kama zeh oleh?
cotton kutna
cotton balls tzemer gefen
cough (noun) shi'ul
  (verb) lehishta'el
country (state) medina
  (not town) ezor kafri
cousin ben dod (m)/bat doda (f)
crab sartan
cracker kreker

cramp hitkavtzut shririm
crayfish lobster
cream shamenet
   whipped cream katzefet
credit card kartis ashrai
crew tzevet
crowded tzafuf
cruise shayit
crutches kabayim
cry *(weep)* livkot
   (shout) litz'ok
cucumber melafefon
cufflinks kaftor кнafatim
cup sefel
curlers rolim
curls taltalim
curry kari
curtain vilon
customs meкнes
cut *(noun: injury)* srita
   (verb) laкнtoкн

dad aba
dairy *(adj.)* кнalavi
   dairy products mutzray кнalav
damp laкн
dance *(noun)* rikud
dangerous mesukan
dark *(color)* keheh
   (night) кнashuкн
date *(meeting)* pgisha
   (fruit) tamar
daughter bat
day yom
dead met
Dead Sea yam ha-melaкн
deaf кнeresh
dear yakar
deck chair kiseh noaкн
deep amok
deliberately be-кнavana
dentist rofeh shinayim

dentures shinayim totavot
deny lehakкнish
   I deny it ani makкнish *(m)/*
   makкнisha *(f)* et zeh
deodorant de'odorant
department store кнanut kolbo
departure yetzi'a, aziva
desert midbar
develop *(film)* lefateaкн
diamond yahalom
diaper кнitul
diarrhea shilshul
diary yoman
dictionary milon
die lamut
diesel dizel
different: that's different zeh shoneh
   I'd like a different one ani rotzeh *(m)/*
   rotza *(f)* mashehu shoneh
difficult kasheh
dining car kron mis'ada
dining room кнadar oкнel
directory *(telephone)*
   madriкн telefon
dirty melukнlaкн
disabled neкнeh
dishwashing liquid sabon kelim
distributor *(car)* mafleg
dive *(verb)* litzlol
diving board keresh kfitza
divorced garush *(m)/*grusha *(f)*
do la'asot
doctor rofeh
document mismaкн
dog kelev
doll buba
dollar dolar
donkey кнamor
door delet
double room кнeder zugi
doughnut sufganya
down lemata
dress simla

drink (*noun*) mashkeh
  (*verb*) lishtot
  what would you like to drink?
  ma tishteh (*to a man*)/tishti? (*to a woman*)
drinking water may shtiya
drive (*verb*) linhog
driver nehag (*m*)/naheget (*f*)
driver's license rishayon nehiga
driving regulations кнukay ha-tnu'a
drugstore bayt mirkaкнat
drunk shikor
dry yavesh
dry cleaner nikui yavesh
during bemesheкн
dust cloth matlit avak
duty-free duty free

each (*every*) kol eкнad
  twenty shekels each esrim shekel
  le'eкнad
ear ozen
  ears oznayim
early mukdam
earrings agilim
east mizraкн
easy kal
eat le'eкнol
egg baytza
eggplant кнatzil
Egypt mitzrayim
Egyptian (*man, adj.*) mitzri
  (*woman*) mitzrit
either: either of them zeh o zeh
  either . . . or . . . o . . . o . . .
elastic gamish
elbow marpek
electric кнashmali
electricity кнashmal
elevator ma'alit
else: something else mashehu aкнer
  someone else mishehu aкнer
  somewhere else makom aкнer

embarrassing meviкн
embassy shagrirut
embroidery rikma
emerald izmargad
emergency кнerum
empty rayk
end sof
engaged (*couple*) me'oras
engine (*car*) mano'a
England anglia
English angli
  (*language*) anglit
Englishman angli
Englishwoman angliya
enlargement hagdala
enough maspik, dai
entertainment bidur
entrance knisa
envelope ma'atafa
eraser maкнak
escalator madregot na'ot
especially bimyuкнad
evening erev
every kol
everyone kulam
everything ha-kol
everywhere be-кнol makom
example dugma
  for example le-dugma
excellent metzuyan
excess baggage mit'an odef
exchange (*verb*) lehaкнlif
exchange rate sha'ar кнalifin
excursion siyur
excuse: excuse me!
  (*to get attention*) sliкнa!
  excuse me? sliкнa?
exit yetzi'a
expensive yakar
eye ayin
  eyes aynayim
eyedrops tipot aynayim

face panim

faint (unclear) metushtash
   (verb) lehit'alef
   to feel faint lehargish кНulsha

fair (carnival) yarid
   it's not fair zeh lo hogen

false teeth ktarim

family mishpaкНa

fan (ventilator) me'avrer
   (enthusiast) ma'aritz (m)/
   ma'aritza (f)
   (sports) ohed (m)/ohedet (f)

fan belt retzu'at ivrur

far: how far is . . .?
   ma ha-merкНak le-. . .?

fare meкНir nesi'a

farm meshek

farmer кНaklai

fashion ofna

fast maher

fat (adj.) shamen

father av

faucet berez

fax (noun) fax
   (verb) lishloaкН fax

feel (touch) laga'at
   I feel hot кНam li
   I feel like . . . mitкНashek li . . .
   I don't feel well ra li

feet kapot raglayim

felt-tip pen tush

ferry ma'aboret

fever кНom gavoha

fiancé arus

fiancée arusa

field sadeh

figs te'enim

filling (tooth) stima
   (sandwich, etc.) milui

filter filter

finger etzba

fire esh
   (blaze) srefa

fire extinguisher maкНshir kibui esh

fireworks zikuk

first rishon

first aid ezra rishona

first floor koma rishona

first name shem prati

fish dag

fishing ladug
   to go fishing latzet ladug

fishing rod кНaka

fish market moкНer dagim

flag degel

flash (camera) flesh

flashlight panas

flat shatuaкН

flat tire pancher

flavor ta'am

flea par'osh
   flea market shuk ha-pishpeshim

flight tisa

flight attendant (m) dayal

flip-flops kafkafim

flippers snapirim

flour kemaкН

flower peraкН

flu shapa'at

flute кНalil

fly (noun: insect) zvuv
   (verb: plane) latus

fog arafel

folk music musikat folklor

food oкНel

food poisoning har'alat kayva

foot kaf regel

for bishvil, le-. . .
   for me bishvili
   what for? bishvil ma?
   for a week le-shavu'a

foreigner zar (m)/zara (f)

forest ya'ar

fork mazleg

fortnight shvu'ayim

fountain pen et nove'a

FOU GUI

fourth revi'i
fracture shever
France tzorfat
free khofshi
  (no cost) khinam
freezer makpi
French fries chips
friend khaver (m)/khavera (f)
friendly yediduti
front: in front of . . . lifnay . . .
frost kfor
fruit (singular) pri
  (plural) payrot
fruit juice mitz payrot
fry letagen
frying pan makhvat
full maleh
  I'm full ani maleh (m)/mele'a (f)
funnel (for pouring) mashpekh
funny (amusing) matzkhik
  (odd) muzar
furniture rahitim

Galilee galil
  Sea of Galilee kineret
garage musakh
garbage ashpa
garden gina
garlic shum
gas delek
gas station takhanat delek
gay (homosexual) homosexual (m)/lesbit (f)
gear mahalakh, hilukh
gearshift yadit hilukhim
Germany germania
get (fetch) lehavi
  have you got . . .?
  yesh lekha . . .? (to a man)/
  lakh . . .? (to a woman)
  to get the train litpos et ha-rakevet
  we get back tomorrow anakhnu
  khozrim makhar

to get something back lekabel
be-khazara
to get in lehikanes
  (arrive) lehagi'a
to get out latzet
to get up (rise) lakum
gift matana
gin jin
girl yalda
  (older) na'ara
girlfriend khavera
give latet
glad sameakh
  I'm glad ani sameakh (m)/
  smekha (f)
glass (material) zekhukhit
  (for drinking) kos
glasses mishkafayim
glossy prints hadpasot mavrikot
gloves kfafot
glue devek
goggles mishkafay skhiya
gold zahav
good tov
  good! tov me'od!
good-bye shalom
  (see you) lehitra'ot
government memshala
granddaughter nekhda
grandfather saba
grandmother savta
grandson nekhed
grapes anavim
grass desheh
gray afor
Great Britain britania
green yarok
grocery store makolet
ground floor komat karka
guarantee (noun) arvut
  (verb: promise) lehavtiakh
guard shomer (m)/shomeret (f)
guidebook madrikh

123

guitar gitara
gun (rifle) roveh
  (pistol) ekdakн

Haifa кнaifa
hair say'ar
haircut tisporet
hairdresser sapar (m)/saparit (f)
hair dryer mayabesh say'ar
hair spray spray la-say'ar
half кнatzi
  half an hour кнatzi sha'a
hamburger hamburger
hammer patish
hand yad
handbag tik yad
hand brake ma'atzor yad
handkerchief mitpaкнat af
handle (door) yadit
handsome na'eh
hangover heng over
happy me'ushar
harbor namal
hard kasheh
hard contact lenses adashot maga kashot
hardware store кнanut klay bayit
hat kova
have: I have a . . . yesh li . . .
  I don't have a . . . ayn li . . .
  can I have a . . .?
  efshar lekabel . . . ?
  have you got a . . .?
  yesh lekнa . . .? (to a man)/
  laкн . . .? (to a woman)
  I have to . . . ani tzariкн (m)/
  tzriкнa (f) le-. . .
  I have to go now ani tzariкн (m)/
  tzriкнa (f) laleкнet aкнshav
hay fever kadaкнat ha-shaкнat
he hu
head rosh
headache ke'ev rosh

headlights panasim kidmiyim
hear lishmo'a
hearing aid maкнshir shmi'a
heart lev
heart attack hetkef lev
heating кнimum
heavy kaved
Hebrew ivrit
heel akev
hello shalom
help (noun) ezra
  (verb) la'azor
  help! hatzilu!
her: it's for her zeh bishvila
  give it to her ten (to a man)/
  tni (to a woman) la et zeh
  her house ha-bayit shela
  her shoes ha'na'alayim shela
  it's hers zeh shela
high gavoha
highway kvish mahir
hill giv'a
him: it's for him zeh bishvilo
  give it to him ten (to a man)/
  tni (to a woman) lo et zeh
his: his house ha-bayit shelo
  his shoes ha-na'alayim shelo
  it's his zeh shelo
history historia
hitchhike la'atzor trempim
hobby takнbiv
holiday (festival) кнag
Holland holand
Holy Land eretz ha-kodesh
honest yashar
honey dvash
honeymoon yeraкн dvash
hood (car) miкнseh mano'a
horn (car) tzofar
  (animal) keren
horrible ayom
hospital bayt кнolim
hotel malon

hour sha'a
house bayit
how? ayкн?, ma?
   how do I get there? ayкн lehagi'a lesham?
   how is he? ma shlomo?
hungry: I'm hungry ani ra'ev (m)/ re'eva (f)
hurry: I'm in a hurry ani memaher (m)/ memaheret (f)
husband ba'al
   my husband/her husband ba'ali/ba'ala

I ani
ice keraкн
ice cream glida
ice cube kubiyat keraкн
ice pop kartiv
if im
ignition hatzata
ill кноleh
immediately miyad
impossible bilti efshari
in be-. . . , ba-. . .
   in English be-anglit
   in the hotel ba-malon
indigestion kilkul kayva
inexpensive zol
infection zihum
information mayda
injection zrika
injury petzi'a
ink dio
inner tube pnimit
insect repellent taкнshir neged yatushim
insomnia neduday shayna
insurance bituaкн
interesting me'anyen
interpret letargem
invitation hazmana
Ireland irland
Irish iri

Irishman iri
Irishwoman irit
iron (noun) maghetz
is: he is . . ./she is . . ./it is . . . hu . . ./hi . . ./zeh . . .
Islam islam
island 'ee
Israel yisra'el
Israeli (man, adj.) yisra'eli (woman) yisra'elit
   the Israelis ha-yisra'elim
it zeh
itch (noun) gerud
   it itches zeh megared

jacket (coat) me'il (suit) zнaket
Jaffa yafo
jam riba
jazz jaz
jealous mekaneh
jeans jins
jellyfish meduza
Jerusalem yerushalayim
Jesus yeshu
Jew yehudi (m)/yehudiya (f)
jewelry store кнanut taкнshitim
Jewish yehudi
job (work) avoda (employment, project) job
jog (verb) larutz
   to go for a jog latzet le-joging
joke bdiкнa
Jordan (river, state) yarden
Jordanian (man, adj.) yardeni (woman) yardenit
Judaism yahadut
just: it's just arrived zeh karega higi'a
   I've just one left nish'ar li rak eкнad
   just two rak shnayim

key mafte<u>a</u>kн
kibbutz ki<u>butz</u>
kidney kl<u>a</u>ya
kilo <u>ki</u>lo
kilometer kilo<u>me</u>ter
kitchen mit<u>ba</u>kн
knee <u>be</u>reкн
knife sa<u>kin</u>
knit lis<u>rog</u>
know: I don't know
  <u>a</u>ni lo yo<u>de</u>'a (*m*)/
  yo<u>da</u>'at (*f*)
Koran kor<u>an</u>
kosher (*noun*) kash<u>rut</u>
  (*adj.*) ka<u>sher</u>

label ta<u>vit</u>
lace taкн<u>a</u>ra
laces (*of shoe*) sroкн<u>im</u>
lake ag<u>am</u>
lamb (*meat*) <u>ke</u>ves
lamp men<u>o</u>ra
lampshade a<u>hil</u>
land (*noun*) <u>e</u>retz
  (*verb*) linкн<u>ot</u>
language sa<u>fa</u>
large ga<u>dol</u>
last (*final*) aкн<u>a</u>ron
  last week ha-shav<u>u</u>'a ha-aкн<u>a</u>ron
  last month ha-<u>кн</u>odesh ha-aкн<u>a</u>ron
  at last! sof sof!
late: it's getting late kvar me'u<u>кн</u>ar
  the bus is late ha-'<u>o</u>tobus me'a<u>кн</u>er
laugh litz<u>кн</u>ok
laundromat maкн<u>be</u>sa
laundry (*dirty clothes*) kvi<u>sa</u>
laundry detergent av<u>kat</u> kvi<u>sa</u>
laxative meshal<u>shel</u>
lazy atz<u>lan</u>
leaf a<u>leh</u>
leaflet a<u>lon</u>
learn lil<u>mod</u>

leather or
Lebanese (*man, adj.*) leva<u>no</u>ni
  (*woman*) leva<u>no</u>nit
Lebanon leva<u>non</u>
left (*not right*) smol
  there's nothing left lo nish'<u>ar</u> klum
leg re<u>gel</u>
lemon li<u>mon</u>
lemonade limo<u>na</u>da
length <u>o</u>reкн
lens ada<u>sha</u>
less pa<u>кнot</u>
lesson shi'<u>ur</u>
letter mikн<u>tav</u>
lettuce <u>кн</u>asa
library sifri<u>ya</u>
license risha<u>yon</u>
license plate lu<u>кн</u>it zi<u>hui</u>
life <u>кн</u>ay<u>im</u>
lifeguard ma<u>tzil</u> (*m*)/metzi<u>la</u> (*f*)
lift: could you give me a lift?
  ef<u>shar</u> leka<u>bel</u> tremp?
light (*not heavy*) kal
  (*not dark*) ba<u>hir</u>
light meter mad or
lighter ma<u>tzit</u>
lighter fuel ben<u>zin</u> le-ma<u>tzit</u>
like: I like you <u>a</u>ta mo<u>tzeh</u> (*to a man*)/
  at mo<u>tzet</u> (*to a woman*) кнen be'ay<u>nai</u>
  I like swimming <u>a</u>ni o<u>hev</u> (*m*)/
  o<u>he</u>vet (*f*) lis<u>кн</u>ot
  it's like . . . zeh kmo . . .
line (*of people*) tor
  (*to line up*) la'a<u>mod</u> ba-<u>tor</u>
lip balm sfa<u>ton</u> <u>ne</u>ged <u>yo</u>vesh
lipstick sfa<u>ton</u>
liqueur li<u>ker</u>
list reshi<u>ma</u>
liter <u>li</u>ter
litter ash<u>pa</u>
little (*small*) ka<u>tan</u>
  it's a little big zeh ktzat ga<u>dol</u>
  just a little rak ktzat

liver kaved
lobster lobster
lollipop sukaria al makel
long arokh
  how long does it take?
  kama zman zeh yikakh?
lost and found office avaydot
lot: a lot harbeh
loud kol ram
loudly be-kol ram
lounge salon, traklin
  (hotel) lobi
love (noun) ahava
  (verb) le'ehov
lover me'ahev (m)/me'ahevet (f)
low namukh
luck mazal
  good luck! be-hatzlakha!
lunch arukhat tzohorayim

magazine zhurnal
mail do'ar
  (verb) lishloakh
mailbox tayvat mikhtavim,
  tayvat do'ar
mail carrier davar
make (verb) la'asot
make-up mayk ap, ipur
man ish, gever
manager menahel (m)/menahelet (f)
mango mango
map mapa
  a map of Jerusalem mapat
  yerushalayim
marble shayish
margarine margarina
market shuk
marmalade marmelada
married nasui (m)/nesu'a (f)
mascara maskara
mass (church) misa
mast toren

match (light) gafrur
  (sports) miskhak
material (cloth) bad
mattress mizron
maybe ulai
me: it's for me zeh bishvili
  give it to me ten (said to a man)/
  tni (said to a woman) li
meal arukha
meat basar
mechanic mekhona'i
medicine trufa
Mediterranean ha-yam ha-tikhon
meeting pgisha
melon melon
menu tafrit
message hoda'a
midday tzohorayim
middle: in the middle ba-'emtza
  the Middle East ha-mizrakh ha-tikhon
  Middle Eastern mizrakh tikhoni
midnight khatzot
milk khalav
mine: it's mine zeh sheli
mineral water mayim mineraliyim
minute daka
mirror re'i
Miss gveret
mistake ta'ut
  to make a mistake lit'ot
mom ima
monastery minzar
money kesef
month khodesh
monument andarta
moon yareakh
moped katno'a
more od
morning boker
  in the morning ba-boker
mosaic psayfas
Moslem (man, adj.) muslemi
  (woman) muslemit

127

mosque mis<u>gad</u>
mosquito ya<u>tush</u>
mother <u>i</u>ma, em
motorboat <u>si</u>rat ma<u>no</u>'a
motorcycle ofa<u>no</u>'a
mountain har
mouse aкн<u>bar</u>
moustache sa<u>fam</u>
mouth peh
move la<u>zuz</u>
  (house) la'a<u>vor</u> di<u>ra</u>
  don't move! lo la<u>zuz</u>!
movie <u>se</u>ret
movie theater kol<u>no</u>'a
Mr. mar
Mrs. <u>gve</u>ret
Ms. <u>gve</u>ret
much har<u>beh</u>
  not much lo har<u>beh</u>
  much better har<u>beh</u> yo<u>ter</u> tov
  much slower har<u>beh</u> yo<u>ter</u> le'<u>at</u>
mule <u>pe</u>red
museum mu<u>say</u>'on
mushroom pitri<u>ya</u>
music <u>mu</u>sika
musical instrument kli negi<u>na</u>
musician musi<u>ka</u>'i *(m)*/musi<u>ka</u>'it *(f)*
  (player) na<u>gan</u> *(m)*/naga<u>nit</u> *(f)*
mussels tzda<u>fot</u>
mustard кнar<u>dal</u>
my: my bag ha<u>tik</u> she<u>li</u>
  my keys
  ha-mafte<u>кнot</u> she<u>li</u>

nail *(metal)* mas<u>mer</u>
  (finger) tzi<u>po</u>ren
nail file ptzi<u>ra</u>
nail polish lak la-tzipor<u>nay</u>im
name shem
napkin ma<u>pit</u>
narrow tzar
Nazareth natz<u>rat</u>, na<u>tze</u>ret

near le<u>yad</u>, al yad
  near the door le<u>yad</u> ha-<u>de</u>let
  near Boston al yad <u>bos</u>ton
necessary na<u>кнutz</u>
necklace *(metal)* shar<u>she</u>ret
  (beads) maкн<u>ro</u>zet
need *(verb)* lehitzta<u>reкн</u>
  I need . . . a<u>ni</u> tza<u>riкн</u> *(m)*/tzri<u>кнa</u> *(f)* . . .
  there's no need ayn <u>tzo</u>reкн
needle <u>ma</u>кнat
negative *(photo)* nega<u>tiv</u>
neither: neither of them af e<u>кнad</u> me<u>hem</u>
  neither . . . nor . . . lo . . . ve-<u>lo</u> . . .
nephew aкн<u>yan</u>
never af <u>pa</u>'am lo
  I have never been to Jerusalem
  af <u>pa</u>'am lo ha<u>yi</u>ti be-yerusha<u>lay</u>im
new кнa<u>dash</u>
news кнada<u>shot</u>
newspaper i<u>ton</u>
newsstand mo<u>кнer</u> ito<u>nim</u>
New Testament ha-<u>brit</u> ha-кнada<u>sha</u>
New Year's *(Jewish)* rosh ha-sha<u>na</u>
  (Christian) rosh ha-sha<u>na</u> ha-ezra<u>кнit</u>,
  sil<u>ves</u>ter
New Zealand niu zi<u>land</u>
New Zealander *(man)* niu zi<u>lan</u>di/
  (woman) niu zi<u>lan</u>dit
next ha-<u>ba</u>
  next week ha-sha<u>vu</u>'a ha-<u>ba</u>
  what next? ma <u>hal</u>'a?
nice neкн<u>mad</u>
niece aкнya<u>nit</u>
night <u>lai</u>la
nightclub mo'a<u>don</u> <u>lai</u>la
night gown ku<u>to</u>net <u>lai</u>la
night porter sho<u>'er</u> <u>lai</u>la
no *(response)* lo
  there are no . . . ayn . . .
  I have no money ayn li <u>ke</u>sef
noisy ro'<u>esh</u>
north tza<u>fon</u>
Northern Ireland tzfon ir<u>land</u>

nose af
not lo
notebook makHberet
nothing shum davar
novel roman
now akHshav
nowhere shum makom
nudist nudist (m)/nudistit (f)
number mispar
nurse akH (m)/akHot (f)
nut (fruit) egoz
   (for bolt) um

occasionally lif'amim
occupation kibush
   the occupied territories
   ha-shtakHim ha-kvushim
octopus tamnun
of shel
office misrad
often le'itim kroyot
oil shemen
   (for car) neft
ointment mishkHa, krem
OK beseder, o kay
old (person) zaken (m)/zkena (f)
   (object) yashan
   (ancient) atik
   the old city ha-'ir ha-'atika
   the Old Testament ha-tanakH
olive zayit
omelette kHavita
on (on top of) al
   (in operating mode) po'el
one ekHad
onion batzal
only rak
open (verb) liftoakH
   (adj.) patuakH
opposite: opposite the hotel
   mul ha-malon
optician optikai

or o
orange (color) katom
   (fruit) tapuz
orange juice mitz tapuzim
orchestra tizmoret
ordinary (normal) ragil
our shelanu
   our hotel ha-malon shelanu
   it's ours zeh shelanu
out: he's out hu lo nimtza
   to get out latzet hakHutza
outside bakHutz
over me'al
   over there sham
oyster tzdafa

pacifier motzetz
pack kHafisa
   a pack of . . . kHafisat . . .
   pack of cards kHafisat klafim
package kHavila
padlock man'ul
page amud
pain ke'ev
paint (noun) tzeva
pair zug
pajamas pijama
pale kHiver
Palestine palestina, falastin
   (referring to the Land of Israel)
   eretz yisrael
Palestinian (man, adj.) palestinai, falastini
   (woman) palestina'it, falastinit
Palestinians palestina'im, falastinim
palm tree dekel
pancake pankayk
pants mikHnasayim
paper niyar
parcel kHavila
parents horim
park (noun) park
   (verb) lakHanot

parking lights orot tzad
parsley petrozilia
party (celebration) mesiba
　(political) miflaga
pass (driving) la'akof
passenger nose'a (m)/nosa'at (f)
Passover pesaкн
passport darkon
pasta pasta
path shvil
pay leshalem
peace shalom
peach afarsek
peanuts botnim
pear agas
pearl pnina
peas afuna
pedestrian holeкн regel (m)/
　holeкнet regel (f)
peg (clothes) mitleh
pen et
pencil iparon
pencil sharpener meкнaded
peninsula кнatzi 'ee
penknife olar
penpal кнaver la-'et (m)/
　кнavera la-'et (f)
people anashim
pepper pilpel
peppermints sukaryot menta
per: per night le-laila
perfect mushlam
perfume bosem
perhaps ulai
perm permanent
photograph (noun) tatzlum
　(verb) letzalem
photographer tzalam (m)/tzalemet (f)
phrase book siкнon
piano psanter
pickpocket kayas
picnic piknik
piece кнatiкнa

pier ratzif
pill kadur
pillow karit
pilot tayas
pin sika
pine (tree) oren
pineapple ananas
pink varod
pipe (for smoking) mikteret
　(for water) tzinor
pistachio nuts fistuk кнalabi
pizza pitza
place makom
plant tzemaкн
plastic plastik
plastic bag sakit nylon
plate tzalaкнat
platform ratzif
play (theater) maкнazeh
please bevakasha
plug (electrical) teka
　(sink) pkak
pocket kis
poison ra'al
police mishtara
policeman shoter
police station taкнanat mishtara
politics politika
pomegranate rimon
poor ani (m)/aniya (f)
　(bad quality) ra
pop music musikat pop
pork basar lavan
port (harbor) namal
porter (for luggage) sabal
　(hotel) sho'er
possible efshari
postcard gluya
poster poster
post office snif do'ar
potato tapuaкн adama
potato chips chips
poultry off

pound (British money) lira
powder avka
prawn KHasilonim
pretty (beautiful) yafeh
priest komer
print lehadpis
printer madpeset
private prati
problem be'aya
  what's the problem? ma ha-be'aya?
Protestant protestanti (m)/
  protestantit (f)
public (noun) tzibur
  (adj.) tziburi
pull limshoKH
purple sagol
purse arnak
push lidKHof

quality ayKHut
question she'ela
quick (adj.) mahir
  quick! maher!
quiet (adj.) shaket
  quiet! sheket!
quite (fairly) dai
  (fully) me'od

rabbi rav
radiator radyator
radio radio
railroad line mesilat rakevet
rain geshem
raincoat me'il geshem
raisins tzimukim
rare (uncommon) nadir
  (steak) na
rat aKHbarosh
razor blades sakinay giluaKH
read likro
reading lamp menorat kri'a

ready muKHan
receipt kabala
receptionist pkid kabala (m)/
  pkidat kabala (f)
record (music) taklit
  (sports, etc.) si
record player patefon
record store KHanut taklitim
red adom
refreshments kibud
refrigerator mekarer
registered letter miKHtav rashum
relative karov (m)/krova (f)
relax lanuaKH
religion dat
remember lizkor
  I don't remember ani lo zoKHer (m)/
  zoKHeret (f)
rent (verb) liskor
  rent out lehaskir
reservation hazmana
reservation office misrad kartisim
rest (remainder) ha-yeter
  (relax) lanuaKH
restaurant mis'ada
restroom (men's) sherutay gvarim
  (women's) shayrutay nashim
return (come back) laKHazor
  (give back) lehaKHzir
rice orez
rich ashir
right (correct) naKHon
  (direction) yamin
ring (wedding, etc.) taba'at
ripe bashel
river nahar
road (main) kvish
  (street, urban level) reKHov
rock (large) sela
  (small) even
  (music) rok
roll (bread) laKHmanya
roof gag

131

room кнеder
  (space) merкнav, makom panui
rope кнevel
rose vered
round *(circular)* agol
  it's my round акнshav tori
round trip ticket
  kartis haloкн va-shov
rowboat sirat meshotim
rubber gumi
rubber band gumiya
ruby *(stone)* margalit, odem
rug *(mat)* shatiaкн
  (blanket) smiкнa
ruins кнorayot
ruler *(for drawing)* sargel
rum rum
run *(verb)* larutz
runway maslul

Sabbath shabat
sad atzuv
safe batuaкн
  is it safe? zeh batuaкн?
safety pin sikat bitaкнon
sailboat mifrasit
salad salat
salami naknik salami
sale *(at reduced prices)* мекнira
salmon salmon
salt melaкн
same oto ha-. . .
  the same dress ota ha-simla
  the same people otam ha-anashim
  same again, please shuv oto ha-davar,
  bevakasha
sand кнol
sandals sandalim
sand dunes djunot кнol
sandwich sendvich
sanitary napkins taкнboshot intimiyot
sauce rotev

saucepan макнvat
sauna sauna
sausage naknik
say lomar
  what did you say? ma amarta *(to a
  man)*/amart? *(to a woman)*
  how do you say . . . (in Hebrew)?
  aукн omrim (be-'ivrit) . . .?
scarf tza'if
  (head) mitpaкнat rosh
school bayt sefer
scissors misparayim
Scot *(man)* scoti
  (woman) scotit
Scotland scotland
Scottish scoti
screw boreg
screwdriver mavreg
sea yam
seafood payrot yam
seat moshav
seat belt кнagorat betiкнut
second *(of time)* shniya
  (in series) sheni
security bitaкнon
  security forces koкнot ha-bitaкнon
see lir'ot
  I can't see ani lo ro'eh *(m)*/ro'a *(f)*
  I see *(understand)* ani mevin *(m)*/
  mevina *(f)*
sell limkor
separate nifrad
separated be-nifrad
serious retzini
several kama
sew litpor
shampoo shampo
shave: to have a shave
  lehitgaleaкн
shaving cream ketzef giluaкн
shawl shal
she hi
sheet sadin

shell tzedef
sherry sheri
ship sfina
shirt KHultza
shoelaces sroKHay na'alayim
shoe polish mishKHat na'alayim
shoes na'alayim
shopping kniyot
  to go shopping la'asot kniyot
short katzar
shorts miKHnasayim ktzarim
shoulder katef
shower *(bath)* miklaKHat
  (rain) geshem
shrimp KHasilonim
shutter *(camera)* miKHseh adasha
  (window) tris
sick *(ill)* KHoleh
  I feel sick ra li
side *(edge)* tzad, katzeh
sidewalk midraKHa
sights *(tourist)* mar'ot
silk meshi
silver kesef
simple pashut
sing lashir
single *(one)* yaKHid
  (unmarried) ravak *(m)*/ravaka *(f)*
single room KHeder le-yaKHid
sink kior
sister aKHot
skid *(verb)* lehakHalik
skin cleanser takHshir nikui la-or
skirt KHatza'it
sky shamayim
sleep *(noun)* shayna
  (verb) lishon
  to go to sleep laleKHet lishon
sleeping bag sak shayna
sleeping pill kadur shayna
slippers na'alay bayit
slow *(adj.)* iti
small katan

smell *(noun)* reyaKH
  (verb) lehariaKH
smile *(noun)* KHiyuKH
  (verb) lekHayeKH
smoke *(noun)* ashan
  (verb) le'ashen
snack KHatif
snorkel shnorkel
snow sheleg
so kol kaKH
  (thus) kaKH
  so good kol kaKH tov
  not so much lo kol kaKH harbeh
soaking solution *(for contact lenses)*
  tmisat hashraya le-adashot
soccer kaduregel
socks garbayim
soda water soda
soft lenses adashot rakot
soldier KHayal *(m)*/KHayelet *(f)*
somebody mishehu *(m)*/mishehi *(f)*
somehow ayKHshehu
something mashehu
sometimes lif'amim
somewhere ayfo shehu
son ben
song shir
sorry: I'm sorry ani mitzta'er *(m)*/
  mitzta'eret *(f)*
  sorry! sliKHa!
soup marak
south darom
South Africa drom afrika
South African *(man, adj.)* drom afrikai/
  (woman) drom afrikait
souvenir mazkeret
spade *(shovel)* et
spare parts KHalafim
spark plug matzat
speak ledaber
  do you speak . . .?
  ata medaber . . .? *(to a man)*/
  at medaberet . . .? *(to a woman)*

I don't speak Hebrew
ani lo medaber (m)/medaberet (f) ivrit
speed mehirut
speed limit mehirut muteret
speedometer mad mehirut
spider akavish
spinach tered
spoon kaf
sport sport
sprain neka
spring (mechanical) kfitz
(season) aviv
stadium itztadyon
staircase/stairs madregot
stamp bul
stapler shadkhan
star kokhav
(movie) kokhav kolno'a (m)/
kokhevet kolno'a (f)
start (verb) lehatkhil
station takhana
statue pesel
steak stayk
steal lignov
it's been stolen zeh nignav
steering wheel hegeh
(f) dayelet
sting (noun) akitza
(verb) la'akotz
stockings garbayim
stomach beten
stomachache ke'ev beten
stop (verb) la'atzor
(bus stop) takhanat otobus
stop! atzor!
store khanut
storm se'ara
strawberry tut
stream nakhal
street rekhov
string (cord) khut
(guitar, etc.) maytar
stroller eglat yeladim

student student (m)/studentit (f)
stupid tipesh
suburbs parbarim, shkhunot
subway rakevet takhtit
sugar sukar
suit (noun) khalifa
(verb) lehat'im
it suits you zeh mat'im
suitcase mizvada
sun shemesh
sunbathe lehishtazef
sunburn kviyat shemesh
sunflower seeds khamanyot
sunglasses mishkafay shemesh
sunny: it's sunny ha-shemesh
zorakhat
suntan shizuf
suntan lotion shemen shizuf
supermarket supermarket
supplement tosefet
sure: are you sure? ata batuakh? (to a
man)/at betukha? (to a woman)
sure! betakh!, bevadai!
surname shem mishpakha
sweat (noun) zay'a
(verb) lehazi'a
sweater sveder
sweatshirt svetshert
sweet matok
swim liskhot
swimming pool braykhat skhiya
switch meteg
to switch on lehadlik
to switch off lekhabot
synagogue bayt kneset
Syria surya
Syrian (man, adj.) suri
(woman) surit

table shulkhan
taillights orot akhoriyim
take lakakhat

134

takeoff *(of plane)* lehamri
takeout tayk eway
talcum powder talk
talk *(noun)* siкна
  (verb) ledaber
tall gavoha
tampon tampon
tangerine mandarina
tape *(invisible, adhesive)* niyar devek
tea teh
telegram mivrak
telephone *(noun)* telefon
  (verb) letalpen
telephone booth ta telefon
telephone call siкнat telefon
television televizya
temperature temperatura
tent ohel
tent peg yated
than: better than . . . yoter tov
  me'asher . . .
thank *(verb)* lehodot
  thanks toda
  thank you toda raba
that: that bus ha-otobus ha-hu
  that man ha-ish ha-hu
  that woman ha-isha ha-hi
  what's that? ma zeh?
  I think that . . . ani кноshev *(m)/*
    кноshevet *(f)* she-. . .
their: their room ha-кнeder
  shelahem *(m)/*shelahen *(f)*
  their books ha-sfarim shelahem *(m)/*
    shelahen *(f)*
  it's theirs zeh shelahem *(m)/*shelahen *(f)*
them: it's for them zeh bishvilam *(m)/*
  bishvilan *(f)*
  give it to them
  latet et zeh lahem *(m)/*lahen *(f)*
then az
there sham
  there is/are . . . yesh . . .
  is/are there . . .? yesh . . .?

thermos® termos
these: these things ha-dvarim ha-'eleh
  these are mine 'eleh sheli
they hem *(m)/*hen *(f)*
thick aveh
  (liquid) samiкн
thin *(person)* razeh *(m)/*raza *(f)*
  (object) dak
  (liquid) dalil
think laкнashov
  I think so ani кноshev *(m)/*
    кноshevet *(f)* kaкн
  I'll think about it aкнshov al zeh
third shlishi
thirsty: I'm thirsty ani tzameh *(m)/*
  tzme'a *(f)*
this: this bus ha-otobus ha-zeh
  this man haish ha-zeh
  this woman ha-isha ha-zo
  what's this? ma zeh?
  this is Mr. . . . zeh mar . . .
  this is Ms. . . . . zo gveret . . .
those: those things ha-dvarim ha-hem
throat garon
throat pastilles kad(u)ray metzitza
through dereкн
thumbtack na'atz
thunderstorm sufat re'amim
ticket kartis
tie *(noun)* aniva
  (verb) likshor
time zman
  what's the time? ma ha-sha'a?
timetable luaкн zmanim
tip *(money)* tip
  (end) katzeh
tire *(on car)* tzamig
tired ayef
  I feel tired ani ayef *(m)/*ayefa *(f)*
tissues tishu
to: to the US le-arzot habrit
  to the station la-taкнana
  to the doctor la-rofeh

toast tost
tobacco ta<u>bak</u>
today ha<u>yom</u>
together (be-)<u>ya</u>кнad
toilet shayru<u>tim</u>
toilet paper ni<u>yar</u> to'a<u>let</u>
tomato agva<u>niya</u>
tomato juice mitz agvani<u>yot</u>
tomorrow ma<u>кнar</u>
tongue la<u>shon</u>
tonic water may <u>tonic</u>
tonight ha-<u>laila</u>
too (also) gam
  (excessive) mi<u>dai</u>
  too hot кнam mi<u>dai</u>
tooth shen
toothache ke'<u>ev</u> shi<u>nayim</u>
toothbrush mivreshet shi<u>nayim</u>
toothpaste mishкнat shi<u>nayim</u>
tour si<u>yur</u>
tourist ta<u>yar</u> (m)/ta<u>yeret</u> (f)
tourist office lishkat mayda le-tayarim
towel mage<u>vet</u>
tower mig<u>dal</u>
town ir
town hall bayt iriya
toy tza'<u>atzu</u>'a
toystore кнa<u>nut</u> tza'atzu'<u>im</u>
track suit trayning
tractor trak<u>tor</u>
tradition ma<u>soret</u>
traffic tnu'<u>a</u>
traffic jam pkak tnu'<u>a</u>
traffic lights ramzo<u>rim</u>
trailer nig<u>rar</u>
train ra<u>kevet</u>
translate letar<u>gem</u>
transmission (for car) tay<u>vat</u>
  hilu<u>кнim</u>
travel agency sokнnut nesi'ot
traveler's check <u>travelers</u> chekim
tray ma<u>gash</u>
tree etz

trip (journey) nesi'<u>a</u>
truck masa'<u>it</u>
trunk ba<u>gazн</u>
try lena<u>sot</u>
tunnel min<u>hara</u>
Turkey <u>turkia</u>
turn signal макнog
tweezers pint<u>zeta</u>
typewriter меккнo<u>nat</u> kti<u>va</u>

umbrella mit<u>riya</u>
uncle dod
under mita<u>кнat</u>
understand leha<u>vin</u>
  I don't understand
  a<u>ni</u> lo me<u>vin</u> (m)/mevi<u>na</u> (f)
underwear bga<u>dim</u> takнto<u>nim</u>
university univer<u>sita</u>
unmarried lo na<u>sui</u> (m)/lo nesu'<u>a</u> (f)
until ad
unusual (special) mayuкнad
  (out of ordinary) <u>bil</u>ti shig<u>rati</u>
up lema'<u>ala</u>
upward klapay ma'<u>ala</u>
urgent da<u>кнuf</u>
us: it's for us zeh bishvi<u>lenu</u>
  give it to us ten (said to a man)/
  tni (said to a woman) et zeh <u>lanu</u>
use (noun) shi<u>mush</u>
  (verb) lehishta<u>mesh</u>
  it's no use zeh кнa<u>sar</u> si<u>kui</u>
useful shimu<u>shi</u>
usual ra<u>gil</u>
usually be<u>de</u>reкн klal

vacancy (room) makom pa<u>nui</u>
vacation кнuf<u>sha</u>
vacuum cleaner sho'<u>ev</u> a<u>vak</u>
valley <u>emek</u>
valve shas<u>tom</u>
vanilla va<u>nil</u>

vase kad

veal bsar egel

vegetables yerakot

vegetarian (person) tzimkhoni (m)/
tzimkhonit (f)

vehicle kli rekhev

very me'od

view mar'eh, nof

viewfinder aynit

villa vila

village kfar

vinegar khometz

violin kinor

visa viza

visit (noun) bikur
(verb) levaker

visitor (guest) oreakh (m)/orakhat (f)
(tourist) mevaker (m)/mevakeret (f)

vitamin pill kadur vitamin

vodka vodka

voice kol

wait (verb) lekhakot
wait! khakeh! (to a man)/
khaki! (to a woman)

waiter meltzar
waiter! slikha!

waiting room khadar hamtana

waitress meltzarit
waitress! slikha!

Wales wayls

walk (noun: stroll) tiyul
(verb: walk) lalekhet
(stroll) letayel
to go for a walk
lalekhet letayel

wall (of house) kir
(of city) khoma
the Wailing Wall ha-kotel hama'aravi

wallet arnak

war milkhama

wardrobe meltakha

warm kham

was: I was hayiti
he was hu haya
she was hi haita
it was zeh haya

wasp tzir'a

wastebasket pakh ashpa

watch (noun) sha'on
(verb) litzpot

water mayim

waterfall mapal mayim

wave (noun) gal
(verb) lenafnef

we anakhnu

weather mezeg ha-avir

wedding khatuna

week shavu'a

welcome: you're welcome al lo davar

Welsh (man, adj.) welshi
(woman) welshit

were: we were hayinu
you were
(singular) hayita (to a man)/
hayit (to a woman)
(plural) hayitem (to men)/
hayiten (to women)
they were hem hayu

west ma'arav

wet ratuv

what? ma?

wheel galgal

wheelchair kiseh galgalim

when? matai?

where? ayfo?

which? ayzeh? (m)/ayzo? (f)/aylu? (plural)

whiskey viski

white lavan

who? mi?

why? lama?

wide rakhav

wife isha
my wife ishti
his wife ishto

wind ruaкн
windbreaker me'il geshem kal
window кнalon
windshield shimsha kidmit
wine yayin
wine list tafrit yaynot
wing (*of plane*) kanaf
with im
without bli
woman isha
wood (*material*) etz
wool tzemer
word mila
word processor me'abed tamlilim
work (*noun*) avoda
  (*verb*) la'avod
worse haкнi garu'a
wrapping paper niyar ariza
wrench mafteaкн bragim
wrist perek yad
writing paper niyar ktiva
wrong lo naкнon

year shana
yellow tzahov
yes ken
yesterday etmol

yet od
  not yet od lo
yogurt yogurt
you (*singular*) ata (*to a man*)/
  at (*to a woman*)
  (*plural*) atem (*to men or mixed group*)/
  aten (*to women*)
your (*singular*) shelкнa (*to a man*)/
  shelaкн (*to a woman*)
  (*plural*) shelaкнem (*to men or mixed
  group*)/shelaкнen (*to women*)
  your shoes
  ha-na'alayim shelкнa (*to a man*)/
  shelaкн (*to a woman*)
  your book
  ha-sefer shelкнa (*to a man*)/
  shelaкн (*to a woman*)
yours: is this yours?
  zeh shelкнa (*to a man*)/
  shelaкн? (*to a woman*)
youth hostel aкнsanyat no'ar

Zionism tziyonut
Zionist (*man, adj.*) tziyoni
  (*woman*) tziyonit
zipper roкнsan
zoo gan кнayot